Penguin Specials fill a gap. Written by some of today's most exciting and insightful writers, they are short enough to be read in a single sitting – when you're stuck on a train; in your lunch hour; between dinner and bedtime. Specials can provide a thought-provoking opinion, a primer to bring you up to date, or a striking piece of fiction. They are concise, original and affordable.

To browse digital and print Penguin Specials titles, please refer to **penguin.com.au/penguinspecials**

LOWY INSTITUTE

The Lowy Institute is an independent, nonpartisan international policy think tank. The Institute provides high-quality research and distinctive perspectives on the issues and trends shaping Australia's role in the world. The Lowy Institute Papers are peer-reviewed essays and research papers on key international issues affecting Australia and the world.

LOWY INSTITUTE

The Myth of the Asian Century

A LOWY INSTITUTE PAPER

BILAHARI KAUSIKAN

PENGUIN BOOKS

UK | USA | Canada | Ireland | Australia
India | New Zealand | South Africa | China

Penguin Books is part of the Penguin Random House group of companies whose addresses can be found at global.penguinrandomhouse.com

First published by Penguin Books, 2025

Copyright © Lowy Institute for International Policy, 2025

The moral right of the author has been asserted.

All rights reserved. No part of this publication may be reproduced, published, performed in public or communicated to the public in any form or by any means without prior written permission from Penguin Random House Australia Pty Ltd or its authorised licensees.

Penguin Random House values and supports copyright. Copyright fuels creativity, encourages diverse voices, promotes free speech and creates a vibrant culture. Thank you for buying an authorised edition of this book and for complying with copyright laws by not reproducing, scanning or distributing any parts of it in any form without permission. You are supporting writers and allowing Penguin Random House to continue to publish books for every reader. Please note that no part of this book may be used or reproduced in any manner for the purpose of training artificial intelligence technologies or systems.

Cover image by kiszon pascal via Getty Images
Typeset by Midland Typesetters, Australia

Printed and bound in Australia by Griffin Press, an accredited ISO AS/NZS 14001 Environmental Management Systems printer

A catalogue record for this book is available from the National Library of Australia

ISBN 978 1 76135 799 2

penguin.com.au

We at Penguin Random House Australia acknowledge that Aboriginal and Torres Strait Islander peoples are the first storytellers and Traditional Custodians of the land on which we live and work. We honour Aboriginal and Torres Strait Islander peoples' continuous connection to Country, waters, skies and communities. We celebrate Aboriginal and Torres Strait Islander stories, traditions and living cultures; and we pay our respects to Elders past and present.

CONTENTS

Introduction

Asia in the 21st century figures as prominently in global geopolitics and the world economy as Europe once did and America still does. This is an incontrovertible fact. I do not dispute it. Why then do I maintain that the idea of an Asian 21st century is a myth? Essentially because the metaphor – which is, at best, all the 'Asian century' amounts to – obscures much more than it illuminates. By the vividness of the image it evokes, by the insights that unexpected comparisons stimulate, a metaphor ought to add depth to our understanding. But the idea of an 'Asian century' is not particularly useful in advancing understanding of Asia's place in the world and its implications.

Today, a quarter of the way into the 21st century, the phrase has become so familiar and appears so self-evident that it seems there is no more to be said on the subject. But when a metaphor suspends thought because over-use has metastasised it into a trope or cliché, it is not just useless but harmful. The purpose of this Paper is not so much to refute the idea of an Asian 21st century as to unpeel the layers of complexity that the phrase, now taken as almost axiomatic, conceals.

Where and what is 'Asia'? This deceptively simple question has engaged me since the early 1970s when I was an undergraduate at what was then called the University of Singapore (now the National University of Singapore). I wrote my political science honours thesis on 'The Idea of Asia'. I was fortunate that my supervisor, the late Professor Wu Teh Yao, allowed me to indulge my interest in a topic that was not obviously 'political science' as the academic orthodoxy understood the term, using a methodology that was literary and philosophical rather than the quantitative approach favoured in the social sciences.

I came to two main conclusions. I now realise both are rather obvious, indeed commonplace, but at the time they struck me with the force of revelation and, commonplace or not, I have found them useful ever since.

First, from the time the ancient Greeks divided the world they knew into three parts – Europe, Libya (by which they meant the northern parts of Africa), and Asia, none of which conformed to modern continental delineations – geography was never just spatially defined. To some degree, geography has always been politically determined: geopolitics defines geography as much as geography defines geopolitics.

Second, as political concepts serving political purposes, spatial geographical definitions were therefore perpetually contingent and dynamic, involving not always conscious political choices that changed as circumstances and political needs and fashions evolved. As political concepts, geographical terms are not just descriptive but almost always also have strong normative undertones, regardless of whether these are declared or intended.

To J.K. Fairbank and E.O. Reischauer, who published the first edition of their classic *East Asia: Tradition and Transformation* in 1965, East Asia meant primarily China and Japan, although there was some discussion of Korea. This was a concept of East Asia built around a sphere of Chinese cultural influence. While the authors certainly had no agenda except the advancement of knowledge, theirs was nevertheless not a politically neutral idea. The 1978 edition of *Tradition and Transformation* included Vietnam, Taiwan, Korea, Hong Kong, and Singapore, because by then US defeat in Vietnam and the growth of the four 'little dragons' merited more extensive treatment.[1] Still, they were incorporated only as 'The Rim Nations of East Asia', which simultaneously emphasised their place in the Sinosphere and their subordinate status in it.

During the 1980s, an expanded idea of East Asia that included the Muslim and Indianised states of Southeast Asia, and not just those in the Sinosphere, gradually crept into the diplomatic lexicon of the Association of Southeast Asian Nations (ASEAN). Rapid economic growth in Indonesia, Malaysia, Thailand, and the Philippines had begun to blur stark differences between the levels of development of Northeast and Southeast Asia, and hence between the Confucian-influenced states and states shaped by Hindu, Muslim, and Christian influences. This mitigated, even if it did not entirely erase, the subaltern status of the latter three.

Acceptance of this expansion in the meaning of East Asia was facilitated by international recognition of ASEAN as the voice of Southeast Asia due to the leading role it played in mobilising international resistance against the Soviet-supported Vietnamese invasion and occupation of Cambodia during the last decade of the Cold War.[2] After the Cold War ended, the definition of Southeast Asia changed again as ASEAN was enlarged to include former adversaries

Vietnam, Laos, and Cambodia as well as neutral Myanmar, making the clearly Confucian-influenced states the minority. In parallel, the idea of East Asia was stretched as by 2011, the ASEAN-initiated East Asia Summit included India, the United States, Australia, New Zealand, and Russia, countries that by no previous definitions were considered East Asian. Their inclusion was a political choice.

The East Asia Summit is not unique in bending geography to politics. The idea of the Asia-Pacific, conceived after China's reform and opening up in 1978, had generated great optimism about the potential for growing economic links between countries, pushed the idea far westwards across the ocean, and infused it with an overwhelmingly cooperative connotation.[3] By the time APEC (Asia-Pacific Economic Cooperation) was formed in 1989, cooperation was taken for granted. But cooperation with whom? India, which has no Pacific coast but is undoubtedly Asian, is not a member of APEC and has little prospect of becoming one; several Latin American countries that are undoubtedly on the Pacific littoral but are indisputably not Asian, are founding members. APEC summits are still a ritual on the region's diplomatic calendar, yet all but the most inveterate optimist must know that its core agenda of trade liberalisation has slowed, if not entirely stalled, and did so long before Donald Trump became US president.

The Indo-Pacific concept – introduced first by Prime Minister Abe Shinzo of Japan in 2016 but now widely used, including in Europe – encompasses India and South Asia. Its western periphery abuts West Asia, but whether or not the Indo-Pacific includes the Gulf states, which are rediscovering old linkages around and across the Indian Ocean and expanding ties with South and East Asia, is still undetermined. Paradoxically, the Indo-Pacific simultaneously limits if not shrinks the idea of Asia politically even as it geographically links Asia's two key oceans, because all but the ASEAN variant of the Indo-Pacific concept are widely perceived to be at least in some degree directed against China. Using 'Indo-Pacific' instead of 'Asia-Pacific' or vice versa to describe this vast region is to signal a political attitude, even if not a definitive choice.

In starting with a passing reference to the ancient Greeks and fast-forwarding to the Indo-Pacific, I have obviously skipped a lot of history. My aim was not comprehensiveness; it was only to give a sense of how the idea of Asia has mutated over time. But through all its innumerable permutations since antiquity, the essential political purpose of the idea of Asia has remained constant. This is to serve as the quintessential 'other', mainly for the West, but in some of its variants (as in the cases of Fairbank's and Reischauer's idea of East Asia, and in the Indo-Pacific concept), also between Asian countries themselves.

As the 'other', Asia was sometimes admired as a model of government by reason or for its spirituality, coveted as a source of fabulous wealth, feared for its teeming masses or revolutionary fervour, or despised for its backwardness and corruption. Seldom, if ever, was it viewed with indifference. The idea that the 21st century is Asian is firmly within this tradition: welcomed by some, viewed with apprehension by others.

Even this short survey of the mutations of the idea of Asia exposes how the noun 'Asia' and its adjective 'Asian' simplify and conceal the complexities of this vast continent. Neither does 'Asia' or 'Asian' necessarily imply the inclusion of all the 48 countries that the United Nations recognises as 'Asian' or the 54 that belong to its Asia-Pacific regional group. Use of the word 'Asia' is always a selection, and the choice is political and serves political purposes. For example, despite their spatial locations, Israel, Canada, Australia, and New Zealand belong to the UN's Western European and Others Group (WEOG), constituting the 'others'. This emphasises their colonial past and in Israel's case, its rejection by the

Asia-Pacific group to which other Middle Eastern countries belong. Turkey belongs to both WEOG and the Asia-Pacific group.

The contention that the 21st century will be, or already is, Asian is not simply a convenient, politically neutral, simplistic, and overused trope. Implicit in some usages is the idea that China, due to its size, spectacular growth, and increasing global reach, will define Asia's future. The glory days of Japan are over; India is too far behind and internally incoherent to matter much; and the rest, whether 'little dragons' or 'tigers', are too small to make a real difference. So the 'Asia' whose century it now is, can only be China. The corollary is of course that the 'West' – that protean term which is often shorthand for the United States – must be the past. This idea of the Asian 21st century is a more palatable – because less aggressively phrased and seemingly objective – version of the Maoist slogan, resurrected by Chinese President Xi Jinping, of 'the East rising and the West declining'.

The emergence of China as a major global player is certainly one of the most important geopolitical facts of the 20th century alongside the collapse of the Soviet Union. The effects will reverberate through the 21st century and perhaps beyond. China must always be a major part of any story of Asia. The rise of new powers does imply a change in the relative position of previously dominant powers such as the United States. But relative change is not absolute change. Acknowledging that China's association with the idea of the Asian 21st century is warranted is a long way from turning a blind eye to its political use by China, its fellow travellers, and its useful idiots, as a tool to expand influence.

Concerns about Chinese influence operations have grown everywhere. However, the nature of these operations is not well enough understood. All countries conduct influence operations, greatly facilitated by 21st century technologies. What is unique about China is that it deploys its influence operations, whether overt or covert, within the framework of an overarching narrative of China's inevitable and unstoppable rise. This is a form of psychological manipulation that amplifies the techniques and effects of its operations.

Beijing's intention is not just to *direct* behaviour but to *condition* behaviour. China does not just want you to comply with its wishes, it wants you to think in such a way that you will, of your own volition, do what it wants you to do.

There is a pattern to Chinese influence operations. An overly simplified but superficially plausible narrative of China's rise is spread by various means.

For the countries of the Global South, it is claimed that China has never in its long history colonised any country (Vietnamese and Koreans, whose countries have repeatedly been invaded and occupied by China, would strongly disagree, as would Tibetans and Uighurs).

Most people are not familiar with Asian history or interested in international affairs. They do not realise they are being fed over-simplifications, and they swallow them. For the more intellectually sophisticated, inducements or the possibility of coercion are dangled tantalisingly to persuade them to look the other way or play along. These inducements are typically economic (being given special advantage in or being cut off from the Chinese market) or academic (being given special access or denied access to Chinese conferences and sources).

For overseas Chinese, there are explicit appeals to ethnicity, facilitated by the anxieties or pride the global resurgence of identity politics often evokes among minority Chinese communities.

The narratives China propagates, underpinned by its long history and growth story, are mesmerising. China appropriates the idea that the 21st century will be Asian so that it becomes the story of China's rise. It is a powerful tool precisely because it is not a complete fabrication. The idea that the Asian century belongs to China is intended to get us to suspend our critical facilities by instilling a sense of fatalistic inevitability so that all other options seem futile and we will accept false choices forced upon us, primarily that we have to choose between the United States and China and that we better, in our own interests, choose the latter.[4]

After all, if the 21st century is Asian and China is the most authentic manifestation of this idea, only a particularly obtuse individual or country would refuse to get on board. This use of the idea of an Asian 21st century is especially, but certainly not exclusively, attractive to some overseas Chinese communities in Southeast Asia and those a Singapore academic has dubbed 'Born-Again Chinese'.[5]

No country can ignore China or avoid dealing with it. US-China competition will shape 21st-century international relations just as US-Soviet strategic competition shaped the second half of the 20th century. Strategic competition is not just material; a crucial dimension is psychological. It is all the more important, therefore, to inoculate ourselves against mental manipulation. We acquire immunity only if we see China as a balanced whole, with its weaknesses as well as its strengths. Then the illusion of inevitability dissipates, our critical faculties reawaken, and China stands before us still big, still powerful, still growing, but, after all, just another country. To see China whole, we also need to see the idea that the 21st century is Asian in all its complexity and in broad perspective.

This Paper has been written in the belief that critical examination of the idea of an Asian 21st century is the best counter to attempts to mess with our minds. I am not a scholar and this is not a work of academic scholarship. Think of this Paper as an extended op-ed by someone whose opinions have been shaped by almost four decades in the service of his country's foreign policy. But the reader should understand that the only title I now hold is that of Singaporean pensioner, and that these are the ramblings of someone who speaks only for himself.

Singapore is a city-state whose ability to influence events outside its borders is always limited but never completely non-existent. To use what agency a small country may have requires the cultivation of a clinical – indeed cold-blooded – cast of mind. Singapore's first Foreign Minister, Mr S. Rajaratnam, once pointed out that every country has one foreign policy of words and another of deeds: theology and diplomacy. For a small country to confuse theology for diplomacy was, he concluded, as suicidal as 'a nun wandering through a red-light district proclaiming the brotherhood of man'.[6]

I do not know whether the reader will agree with my opinions. I will make my argument in broad strokes so there will be ample room for debate. I do not claim that mine is the last word on this or any subject. But I can unreservedly assure you that in all my time in the Singapore Foreign Service, the thought of preaching in a red-light district has never even fleetingly crossed my mind.

CHAPTER ONE

What's in a century?

In 1988, Deng Xiaoping, then the paramount leader of China, met Rajiv Gandhi, then prime minister of India, and told him: 'In recent years, people have been saying that the next century will be the century of Asia and the Pacific, as if that were sure to be the case. I disagree with this view.'[7]

We need to be reminded of this sobering assessment from China's greatest modern leader because today the idea that the 21st century will be Asian, just as the 20th century was supposed to have been American, is too often regarded as self-evident and thus more often repeated than examined. There have indeed been important global shifts in which 'Asia' has figured prominently. But to attach a geographical label to them conceals much more than it illuminates. The proposition that an 'Asian century' will replace or already has replaced an 'American century' is flawed both factually and in its underlying premises.

'Asia' is too broad a category to have any coherent political or strategic meaning. It is more accurate to say that specific Asian countries or Asian leaders have played major roles in global shifts of power and ideas, and that this has been going on in different ways since the late 19th and early 20th centuries when Imperial Japan first defeated Qing China in 1895 and then defeated Imperial Russia in 1905. It would be tedious to repeat this qualification every time I use the word 'Asia', but readers should bear it in mind.

One of the earliest uses of the phrase 'The Asian Century' that I am aware of is the title of a book, first published in 1956, by the Dutch historian Jan Romein about the rise of nationalism in Asia.[8] But at that time, no Asian country played a global role, politically or economically. All were poor. China isolated itself and was poised to take a 'Great Leap Forward', a shortcut to communist utopia that no one, even other 'socialist' countries, was eager to follow. India had global ambitions but its capabilities were meagre. Japan was still recovering from the Second World War. Although its defeat of Russia in the early 20th century had a significant influence on Asian nationalism, the stigma of its recent militarist past still hung heavy on Japan's reputation. It was not until the 1970s that the soaring Japanese economy again became an inspiration to other Asian countries.

There are serious conceptual and historical difficulties in associating an entire political era or order with any continent. To do so imposes a unity of thought and purpose that often simply does not exist.

The long European 'century' – something like two to three hundred years if dated from the colonial systems that began to take root during the late 17th century, reached full bloom in the 19th century, and lingered on until the second half of the 20th century – was rife with intra-European rivalries. It was those rivalries that often propelled European powers to expand their empires globally.

America's decision to intervene in the First World War in 1917 was decisive in determining the outcome. Without the United States on their side, Britain and France may not have defeated Germany. But although 1917 may have marked the beginning of the end of the European era, a United States divided about its global role soon returned to its own preoccupations, allowing Europe a reprieve of a few more decades.

So when Henry Luce, publisher of the influential *Life* magazine, wrote an editorial entitled

'The American Century' in February 1941, it was still more an exhortation to Americans to play an active role in resisting dictatorships rather than the description of an established American order.[9] If there was indeed an 'American century', it was a short century of about 67 years from December 1941 when the Japanese attack on Pearl Harbor brought the United States into the Second World War, to circa 2008 when the global financial crisis catalysed widespread disillusionment with US-led globalisation, including among many Americans.

Competition and conflict, or at least the possibility of conflict, are inherent characteristics of any system of sovereign states. They are the permanent verities of international relations, rooted in the very concept of sovereignty, the dynamics of interaction between sovereignties, and ultimately in the dark recesses of human nature itself. It is therefore a fundamental mistake to think that any international order or era, whether geographically defined or not, must necessarily be the result of a consensus. In world history, there has seldom been any period of unchallenged international order. More often than not, it was competition over different conceptions of 'order' that defined international relations. Whatever 'order' that existed was either imposed by force or, if that was not possible, shaped by the reality of competition.

The so-called 'American century' was never uncontested. During the Cold War – 40 of the 67 years of the 'American century' – it was the contest between the United States and the Soviet Union, their efforts to reduce the risks of competition, and conflicts between their proxies, that defined international order. The Soviet bloc and China as well as members of the Non-Aligned Movement – the population of more than half the world – rejected key premises of the American order. Even substantial numbers of the populations of the United States and its allies disagreed with what Washington decreed and took their disagreements not just to the ballot box but often to the streets. The Cold War generated many risks and uncertainties, it was sometimes very dangerous, but regardless of which side we identified with or even if we tried or pretended to be non-aligned, for 40 years it was the only 'order' we knew.

Two key pillars of the American-conceived post-Second World War global order – the UN system and the Bretton Woods system – have never really functioned as their founders hoped, although they did and still do useful journeyman service.[10] From their inception, the United Nations and most other post-war institutions became arenas for Cold War contests. The UN system was based on a false premise – that the wartime anti-axis alliance would endure after the axis was defeated – and was handicapped from the start. The World Bank and the International Monetary Fund did somewhat better, but a central premise of the Bretton Woods system was destroyed overnight when President Richard Nixon unilaterally and without warning delinked the US dollar from gold in August 1971.

The harsh reality of competition and conflict was masked by the overwhelming dominance of US power during a short and exceptional period of less than 20 years from 1989, when the Berlin Wall came down, to circa 2008, when the global financial crisis broke out. American ideas alone then seemed to define the international order.

'Globalisation' is the modest name given to that vision of international order. But the temptation to see the end of the Cold War not just as another geopolitical event (albeit of profound consequence) in a historical process with no end but to invest it with universal significance proved irresistible to a certain cast of mind. Some were even arrogant enough to suggest that History itself may have ended.[11]

Of course, events paid no heed to such foolish theories and went rolling bloodily onwards. Despite the dominance of the United States, the norms and rules that America and its allies regarded as the natural order of things did not go unchallenged.

In 1990, Saddam Hussein invaded Kuwait and little more than a decade later, the United States invaded Iraq. Vicious genocidal wars erupted in the Balkans and Rwanda. Islamist jihadists violently disputed the fundamental premises of not just American ideas and values, but of modernity itself. This culminated in the terrorist attacks of 11 September 2001. The 9/11 attacks drew the United States into interminable wars – the longest in American history – in the Middle East. 'Order' has never meant peace.

Even countries that benefited from the international order as America and its allies conceived it never swallowed it whole. We may have used the same phrase – 'rules-based order' – to describe it, but we never meant exactly the same thing by those words. Which rules to emphasise, and how to interpret the rules, were subjects of continual debate. Except at such a high level of generality that they prescribed little of practical significance, there was scant agreement. Most rules, including rights claimed to be universal, were contested. For instance, Singapore, like many other countries in Asia and elsewhere, was much more invested in the economic rules than the political rules and rejected the claim that certain rules granted other countries a voice in how we governed ourselves.[12]

That short, exceptional period of world history was nevertheless extremely beneficial for most of us, particularly in Asia. We grew and prospered during that time. Globalisation was never only an economic concept. As will be explained later, it was also extraordinarily influential in reshaping the dynamics of international relations in ways that survive the passing of that period. But just because it was good for us, and influential, does not make it any less exceptional or more replicable. It is over.

We have returned to a more historically normal period of world history where competition and the ever present possibility of conflict again defines 'order'.

Rivalry between the United States and China, and the wars in Ukraine and Gaza, do not pose any risks that we have not faced before. How are Ukraine or Gaza in principle different from the American invasions of Iraq and Afghanistan or the endemic violence that has devastated the Congo and Sudan, to name just a few examples? The risks and uncertainties we now face are real, but they are what the late US Secretary of Defence Donald Rumsfeld termed 'known unknowns'.

I am constantly surprised by how much resistance this simple and obvious fact arouses in otherwise acute observers of geopolitics. They grew too comfortable during that exceptional period of world history, confused the exceptional for the norm, and clung desperately to the belief that what was good for them was, or ought to be, the natural order of the world. Now, when the fundamental truths of international relations have reasserted themselves, they have been thrown into a state of denial or confusion. Talk about history ending has long receded into embarrassed silence, but shadows of the attitude that spawned such theories linger.

In his conversation with Rajiv Gandhi, Deng Xiaoping argued that aside from the United States, the only countries in the Asia-Pacific that were relatively developed were Japan, the 'four little dragons' of South Korea, Taiwan, Hong Kong, and Singapore, as well as Australia and New Zealand. This was only a small percentage of the region's population, dwarfed by those of China and India. Deng concluded: 'No genuine Asia-Pacific century or Asian century can come until China, India, and other neighbouring countries are developed.'

In the almost four decades since Deng spoke to Gandhi, the Asia-Pacific has grown significantly. Estimates vary, but in 2024 in purchasing power parity (PPP) terms, the Asia-Pacific, excluding the United States, accounted for around 46 per cent of world GDP. If the United States is included, the share rises to 60.7 per cent. In PPP terms, China accounted for about 19.5 per cent of world GDP, India 8.2 per cent, Japan 3.3 per cent, Indonesia 2.3 per cent, South Korea 1.6 per cent, and Australia just under 1 per cent.

Growth and economic weight is, however, not strategic coherence, nor does it lead to collaboration. Not stated explicitly but clear enough in Deng's conversation with Rajiv Gandhi was that China and India would not just have to grow together but work together. In a press article for his first visit to India in 2014, Xi Jinping himself wrote: 'I am confident that *as long as China and India work together*, the Asian century of prosperity and renewal will surely arrive at an early date.' [emphasis added][13]

The opposite happened. Within weeks of Xi's visit, Indian and Chinese forces clashed in the Himalayas. Since 2014, there have been several serious incidents, some resulting in fatalities, on the Sino-Indian Line of Actual Control (LAC). Although tensions have eased, both sides maintain large numbers of troops in the Himalayas and are enhancing their military infrastructure along the LAC.[14] The substantive differences over their border remain unresolved and are unlikely ever to be definitively settled. Stability in the Himalayas is not to be taken for granted.

It is not just the Himalayas. The most active disputes in Asia all involve China: in the East and South China Seas and, most dangerous of all, over Taiwan. China's relations with Japan, both Koreas, Vietnam, and India are historically fraught, as are many other intra-Asian relationships: between Japan and both Koreas, between India and many of its South Asian neighbours, and between several members of ASEAN, including Malaysia and Indonesia with each other and with Singapore, and Thailand with Myanmar and Cambodia, to name just some of the fault lines.

Many of these intra-Asian complications have been mitigated, particularly in Southeast Asia, by ASEAN. None, however, has been erased, and it is unlikely that they can ever be completely wiped clean because they do not just involve differences of interests that could be reconciled but primordial questions of race, language, and religion that trigger visceral responses.

I am not going to discuss any of these disputes or complicated relationships in detail. There are many specialised works on them that the interested reader may consult. But the fact that intra-Asian relationships are not naturally cooperative is a serious limitation to the idea of an 'Asian century' insofar as that requires a minimal level of political coherence, and hence convergence of interests, among Asians. This has never existed except in the imaginations of pan-Asianists of various stripes, from the early Asian nationalists to the present.

Although intra-European relationships were often fraught in the 19th and early 20th centuries, this did not diminish the overall primacy of Europe. Despite their differences, what all European powers had in common was the conviction that they were the natural 'Lords of Human Kind'.[15] This ensured that whatever their differences, Europe had a common interest in preserving the colonial system. But despite their opposition to colonialism, there was no credible unifying idea to bring Asian nationalists together.

'Asia is one' boldly asserted the very first sentence of Kakuzo Okakura's *The Ideals of the East*, published in 1903, one of the earliest attempts to make a case for the unity of Asia.[16] His ideas were not atypical of much early nationalist thought. Across Asia, in Japan, India, and China, thinkers debated, criticised, and cross-fertilised in a rich but ultimately vain intellectual quest for unity.[17] Much as they tried, efforts to find commonality amid Asia's diversity usually dissolved into mystical vapouring about the allegedly superior spirituality of Asia as compared to the West, perhaps a form of psychological compensation for the reality of powerlessness. Today, Okakura is remembered, if he is remembered at all, for his writing on the Japanese tea ceremony and his work overseeing oriental art at Boston's Museum of Fine Arts, worthy but hardly politically weighty matters.

In March and April 1947, with Indian independence only months away, an Asian Relations Conference was convened in New Delhi at the initiative of the Indian Congress Party. Jawaharlal Nehru, who was to become independent India's first prime minister, took on most of the substantive work of chairing the conference. The intention was to begin to address common problems. It was attended by 28 Asian delegations, only a handful of which were from independent countries. Among them were delegations from China, then in the end stages of civil war, Soviet Central Asia and the Caucasus, as well as Egypt and a Jewish delegation from Palestine. The conference opened with hopeful speeches, but from the outset was bedevilled by many of the issues that still plague Asia. Congress' political rival, Muhammad Ali Jinnah's Muslim League, tried unsuccessfully to instigate a boycott by Muslim delegations; China clashed with the host, India, over its invitation to Tibet; Egypt and the Jewish delegation squabbled because the latter called Palestine their Holy Land. It took all of Nehru's diplomatic skills to preserve a veneer of solidarity, and the conference ended on a mildly optimistic note with the announcement that a second conference would be held in China in two years' time. It never took place.[18]

The Asian nationalist revolt against European colonialism provided mutual inspiration and some sense of common purpose, but not as much cooperation as the early nationalists hoped. The convening of the 1947 Asian Relations Conference in the face of many daunting political and logistical challenges was a symbol of nationalist hopes, but once convened, its dynamics betrayed that shared hope was a tenuous basis for common action or even to just sustain solidarity. Today, when every Asian country is independent, Asian nationalisms – the plural is crucial – are more often than not directed against each other. This is not an inconsequential fact: since the early 20th century, nationalism has proven to be by far the most powerful and enduring idea in Asia, outlasting or bending ideologies of both Left and Right to its service. Nationalism will continue to be the single most important influence on the evolution of the idea of an Asian century.

CHAPTER TWO

How did Asia grow?

Nothing I have said so far is intended to denigrate the Asian growth story upon which the idea of an Asian 21st century ultimately rests or to suggest that it is illusory. It is a real and inspiring story. There is no other example in history of so many people – perhaps a billion or more – lifted out of extreme poverty in about 40 years since the 1980s.

Why did Asia succeed? The essential reason is, I think, simple. While many, perhaps every, country on every continent in what we now call the Global South *talks* about prioritising economic development, few countries really mean it – their priorities are too often elsewhere. Almost all the countries that really meant it were in Asia. This is the real 'Asian miracle'. Much of what the World Bank described in a widely cited 1993 report on the East Asian miracle was to my mind standard economic policies open to all countries in all continents. But most countries in, say, Africa or Latin America, stagnated or grew only fitfully.[19] What set apart those Asian countries that achieved high growth rates from the 1960s onwards was the determined and sustained commitment of their political leaderships to growth. With this laser-like focus on development, the conflicts and tensions Asia endured during that period may have slowed growth but never derailed it.[20]

However, economic success is not vouchsafed by God to any Asian country. Asia will probably still grow faster than other regions, but the time of 'miracles' is over.

Economic success has made domestic politics in several key Asian countries more complicated and a hinderance to the single-minded focus that had hitherto characterised their approach to economic development. During its heyday, growth was often at the expense of other societal goals that can no longer be ignored. New political and other demands have risen from previously passive populations and cannot be managed by old methods. It pleases some Western commentators to call this the spread of 'democracy'. But the sad fact is that many Western democracies have been incapable of dealing effectively with their economic problems precisely because they are democracies and thus subject to conflicting public pressures. Some variant of this phenomenon – perhaps a more serious one – has also manifested in authoritarian polities, notably China. Economic and other headwinds are rising across Asia.[21] Here too we are, sadly, witnessing what could be called a return to normalcy in Asia.

But not the kind of 'normalcy' that my former colleague, Kishore Mahbubani, one of the most ardent promoters of the 'Asian century', had in mind when he argued that 'the last two centuries of Western domination of world history have been a major historical aberration. From the years 1 to 1820, the two largest economies of the world were those of China and India . . . All historical aberrations come to a natural end. Therefore the Asian Century is irresistible and unstoppable.'[22]

Mahbubani may well be right that China and India were the world's largest economies centuries ago. But of what relevance is that today? It is a debating point that sounds clever but proves nothing.

To conceive of the 'Asian century' as the recovery of Asia's historical place in the world prior to contact with the West resonates with the Chinese Communist Party's (CCP) legitimating narrative of 'humiliation', 'rejuvenation', and achieving the 'China Dream'. In essence, this is a narrative of restoring past glories and China's place at the apex of an Asian hierarchy that Beijing imagines China occupied before the West brought it low. That narrative underpins China's claim that it has, in the words of former Foreign Minister Qin Gang, 'shattered the myth that modernisation is Westernisation'.[23]

Qin has fallen out of favour, but he was only echoing Xi Jinping's grandiloquent boast at the 19th National Congress in 2017 that China was 'blazing a new trail for other developing countries to achieve modernisation. It offers a new option for other countries and nations who want to speed up their development while preserving their independence; and it offers Chinese wisdom and a Chinese approach to solving the problems facing mankind.'[24]

The claim of a unique Chinese path to modernisation is no mere boast. It is central to China's attempt to appropriate the idea of an Asian century for its own ends and underpins Xi's Global Civilisational Initiative. But the claim is at best only partially true. The issue confronting the non-Western world since contact with the West has been adaptation to Western-defined modernity. The most successful examples of adaptation have all been in Asia. China's general development trajectory is not essentially different from that of Japan, South Korea, Singapore, Taiwan, India, Vietnam, Malaysia, Thailand, or any other example of successful modernisation and development.

The idea of the Asian century as recovery of the past ignores the profound changes the West has wrought on Asia through centuries of interaction. Modernisation has always entailed westernisation (spelt with a lower case 'w') and never Westernisation (spelt with an upper case 'W'). Modernisation has always involved adapting the ideas and techniques of Western industrial society to local conditions for a very simple reason: until Japan developed after the Meiji Restoration, all modern industrial societies were Western. Traditional Asian societies were not static; they changed over time and could invent and innovate, but until contact with the West, they had no concept of modernity as we now understand the term.

Initially, the only models available to Asian modernisers were European or American. Asian countries could choose between the capitalist US-European model, which stressed the market economy and liberal democracy based on the individual, or the communist Soviet-Russian model, which emphasised the planned economy and a 'people's democracy' in which the individual is subordinated to the vanguard party.

After the overthrow of the Qing Dynasty in 1911, republicanism (the US-European model) and communism (the Soviet-Russian model) contended to replace traditional Chinese political forms as the best road to reclaim the 'wealth and power' China believed it had lost to the West. Communism emerged victorious in 1949 and defines the Chinese polity to this day. As an ideology, communism no longer has much attraction in China – there are probably more believers in class struggle in Western universities than in the CCP – but China is still unmistakably a Leninist state led by a vanguard party, an identity that Xi has enhanced ever since he assumed power. Adding the phrase 'with Chinese characteristics' to China's model and trying to enlist Confucianism to support the CCP's agenda, as Xi has attempted, does not negate the strong Western influence on China. Marx, Engels, and Lenin are not ancient Chinese sages.

Whichever model they chose, in all Asian countries there were always local cultural, sociological, and historical particularities that could not be ignored. From Meiji Japan to present-day Singapore, the successful Asian modernisers have never been mere carbon copies of either Western model. They are all adaptations to local conditions and none developed in exact conformity with Western modernisation theories, although the United States often found it convenient to pretend otherwise where its allies and friends were concerned.

To conceive of the 'Asian century' as reclaiming a place held in the past ignores the most important reason for Asia's economic success. If Asian countries have generally adapted better to Western-defined modernity and thus grown faster than countries in other non-Western regions, it is because they have more thoroughly enmeshed themselves into the world economy and occupied some of the most important nodes in it. China itself is the prime example.

During the Cold War, the United States opened its markets to allies and friends not out of altruism but from strategic necessity. Today, when great-power competition again defines international relations, it has become common to refer to US-China strategic competition as a 'new Cold War'. This evokes a superficially plausible but in fact inappropriate historical analogy. To describe the US-China contest as a Cold War is to misrepresent the essential nature of their competition and the contemporary world economy.

The US-Soviet Cold War was an existential struggle between two systems based on fundamentally different principles and connected with each other only at their margins. Economic links between the United States and the Soviet Union were inconsequential. The prospect of nuclear destruction tempered their rivalry, with violence being exercised through proxies, and Washington and Moscow eventually reaching peaceful co-existence and then détente. Still, to its very end the in-principle goal of US-Soviet competition was for one system to replace the other because it would prove to be the superior means of organising industrial society and providing a better life for their peoples. This was what Nikita Khrushchev meant in 1956 when he told a group of Western ambassadors during a reception at the Polish embassy in Moscow that 'we will bury you'.[25]

That argument is definitively settled. We know who buried whom. During the Cold War, the differences between the market economies of the West and the planned economies of the Soviet bloc were fundamental. But after the collapse of the Soviet Union and Deng Xiaoping's reform and opening up, China, like all economies, is now a mixed economy. The difference between the United States (and other Western economies) and China lies in the balance between the market and state-controlled elements in their systems (though the West prefers to call state control 'regulation'). Differences in the balance between these elements are still important, as we shall see when we discuss China, but not as stark or fundamental as those that existed between capitalism and communism during the US-Soviet Cold War. The United States and China are certainly rivals. But who can today seriously hope or fear that communism will replace capitalism?

An even more crucial difference is that the Soviet Union, apart from the energy sector, never had much of an international economic influence outside its own bloc. But the United States and China are today both vital components of a single global system, intimately enmeshed with each other and the rest of the world by a web of supply chains of a scope, density, and complexity that is historically unprecedented.

In 1919, the economist John Maynard Keynes wrote of an inhabitant of London being able to lie in bed, sipping his morning tea, and ordering by telephone 'products of the whole earth'.[26] The operative word in this famous passage is 'products'. The supply chains that exist today are many times removed from finished 'products' and have created a far more complex global economic system.

The classical Ricardian theory of trade based on comparative advantage envisaged countries specialising in and exchanging goods for which they had a production advantage. Beef, say, for one country, wine for another, and beds for a third. The exchange of beef, wine, and beds would maximise the welfare of all three countries, with citizens of all three living happily ever after, lying drunk and with full stomachs on comfortable beds.

This is what Keynes meant when he talked about 'products' – something a consumer can immediately eat, drink, or use. Estimates vary, but today, intermediate goods and services – that is to say, components of the final products and not something you can immediately eat, drink, or use – account for at least half of world trade and perhaps as much as 70 per cent.

The metaphor of a 'chain' understates the complexity of this system because a chain is a simple linear structure. A more appropriate metaphor is the intricate root system of a tree leading to its trunk, and then leading in turn to branches, twigs, and the capillaries of leaves. Today, the global economic system comprises a thick forest of trees whose roots and branches are intertwined with each other across continents. This 'forest' of supply chains is what distinguishes 21st-century interdependence from earlier periods of interdependence such as that which Keynes described.

The seeds of that forest were planted by the United States and rapidly spread across the globe during the short, exceptional period of world history after Cold War barriers came down. There is ample historical experience to show that interdependence does not prevent conflict. But as the next chapter will argue, the new 21st-century interdependence nevertheless has had a profound and, I think, permanent influence on the dynamics of competition and the calculation of risks.

The global forest has blurred conventional boundaries between countries and continents. When a product is designed in one country by teams from around the world and assembled in another country from components sourced from scores of countries across continents, which country's product is it? Asia is more deeply integrated into this global forest than other regions and its most important nodes are located in Asia. As the previous chapter has emphasised, nationalisms of various kinds are also an inescapable part of Asian reality. China's status as the 'factory of the world' and its disputes in the Himalayas, the East and South China Seas, and over Taiwan, give the interaction between Chinese nationalism and other Asian nationalisms a special significance. How will the tensions between geo-economics and Asian nationalisms play out?

CHAPTER THREE

'Asia' without America?

Asia's growth rests on foundations of stability laid by the United States. Insofar as modern Asia is characterised by economic success, there could have been no 'Asian century' without America. The very terms 'Asia-Pacific' and 'Indo-Pacific', and forums such as the East Asia Summit and APEC, recognise that the United States is part of Asia in this sense. The overarching question is whether the system I have dubbed the global forest will survive the resurgence of great-power competition and an American president who is not only uncommitted to the post-war international order but seems to delight in disruption.

The global forest that defines 21st-century interdependence has reshaped the dynamics of major-power competition between the United

States and China. It is no longer a binary competition *between* two separate systems organised on diametrically opposed principles, as it was between the United States and the Soviet Union. Two mixed economies are now engaged in a complex competition *within* a single global system.

The dynamics of competition within a system are fundamentally different from competition between systems because the former is not existential; it is not about one system replacing another. Instead, competition within a system is about using the complexities of interdependence as tools of competition: positioning yourself to continue to benefit from interdependence and mitigating your vulnerabilities while exploiting those of your rival. It is not likely to end in as neat and definitive a dénouement as did US-Soviet competition.

Competition within a system may be as fierce as competition between systems. Beijing is an ambitious peer competitor that may wish to dominate the system and relegate the United States to subordinate status, or the United States may wish to preserve its preeminent status and suppress or slow China's rise. But these are not existential goals. Labelling the competition as one between 'democracy' and 'authoritarianism', as some in the West are wont to do, is not merely simplistic – both are protean terms with many variants, and not everyone regards Western democracies with unqualified admiration or recoils in horror from every variant of authoritarianism – but focuses on the peripheral rather than the essential. One type of mixed economy cannot replace another type of mixed economy without undermining the entire system and risking grievous harm to itself. The fact that the political institutions and practices of these mixed economies are different is a second-order issue.

China is arguably the chief beneficiary of the global forest. There is no strong reason for Beijing to seek entirely new arrangements even assuming it has the ability to do so. Beijing's claims in the Himalayas and in the East and South China Seas are revanchist, as are its designs over Taiwan. But to label China a 'revisionist power' or a 'systemic competitor' is an overstatement.

Both the United States and China are uncomfortable with the global forest because their interdependence exposes their vulnerabilities. Both have tried to mitigate them: America and its allies by denying China key technologies and by diversifying to reduce dependence on China; China by trying to become more technologically self-reliant and placing more emphasis on domestic household consumption to drive growth. I doubt either strategy will succeed, at least not to the extent the United States and China may hope.

On 2 April 2025, Donald Trump declared 'Liberation Day' and slapped high tariffs on almost every country in the world, with a baseline of ten per cent. He seems to regard tariffs as a kind of Swiss Army Knife, a universal tool to achieve multiple goals: to protect national security (illegal immigration and fentanyl smuggling), gain negotiating leverage, raise revenue, reduce the deficit in goods, and as a form of industrial policy to bring manufacturing back to the United States. Taken individually, these are not illogical goals and he may achieve partial success. Countries are queuing up to cut deals with him. The question is whether the ultimate cost of tariffs outweighs the benefits, assuming that the goals can be achieved, particularly the diversification of supply chains to bring manufacturing back to the United States. Some major investments into the United States have been announced. But manufacturing left the United States for a variety of reasons, not just lower costs abroad.

Diversification of supply chains is easier said than done – it is not a straightforward matter of merely moving plants from China back to the United States or to friendly countries. To replicate the scale of manufacturing in China, entire manufacturing ecosystems will have to be recreated, supported by infrastructure and labour with the requisite skills. Even if this is attempted, it will take a long time to have a significant effect. Partial diversion of supply chains has already occurred and there will undoubtedly be more. The system may bifurcate in certain domains, particularly in areas of technology with security implications. This will place stresses on globalisation. But apocalyptic scenarios of this exceptionally complex global system dividing across all sectors into two separate systems, as existed during the US-Soviet Cold War, lack credibility. Globalisation will become patchy and slow down, but will not be reversed.

However deep their concerns about China and no matter how much pressure Washington exerts on them, even the closest American ally is never going to cut itself off from China politically or economically. European Commission President Ursula von der Leyen put it neatly when she said the European Union will de-risk economic relations with China but not decouple from China. The same holds true for America's Asian allies. They will de-risk their economic relations with China and take other, perhaps largely performative, measures to assuage the United States about their economic ties with China, but will never substantively cut ties.

For China, self-reliance is a comforting slogan but not a viable strategy in a densely interconnected world. Another Chinese slogan – 'dual circulation' – acknowledges Beijing's inability to separate itself from the world. Systemic overcapacity in key sectors of the Chinese economy makes self-reliance well-nigh impossible without serious economic risk. Beijing has been trying to raise domestic consumption for more than a decade, but the rate has flattened out and is still below 40 per cent of GDP (it is about 68 per cent in the United States). It remains to be seen whether the latest round of measures intended to boost domestic demand will prove any more successful than earlier attempts.

Despite all the tensions and disruptions, the total volume of US-China trade was more than US$582.5 billion in 2024. Between 2017, when Trump took office, and 2023, US-China trade fluctuated from US$635 billion in 2017 to US$574.6 billion in 2023, reaching a high of US$690.3 billion in 2022 and never falling lower than US$555.5 billion in 2019. Bearing in mind that 2020 and 2021 were pandemic years, this does not suggest any significant US-China 'decoupling'.

High tariff levels have begun to reduce the volume of US-China trade, to the detriment of both parties. But China has no real alternative to the West, and specifically the United States, for critical technologies and its most important markets. The application of Chinese advances in new fields such as artificial intelligence (AI) still largely rest on Western foundational technologies. The Global South may provide resources and markets for some Chinese products but is not an adequate substitute. It is an open question whether China's closest partners in the Global South are assets or liabilities; a Pakistan constantly teetering on the brink of state failure and some debt-ridden African states come to mind.

Russia is China's only partner of any strategic weight that shares its distrust of the West, but is Moscow an asset or a liability? Again, the fact that it is difficult to give a clear answer to the question is an answer of sorts. Russia is no substitute for the West. Apart from the defence industry sector, Russia is still very largely a resource-based economy, much more akin to a developing nation than an advanced industrial one. In any case, for demographic reasons its long-term future is bleak.

The geopolitics of high-end semiconductors is another illustration of how complete decoupling of the global system is highly improbable. High-end semiconductors are a serious vulnerability for China.[27] All the most critical nodes in the semiconductor supply chain are held by the United States and its allies and friends. But China is about 40 per cent of the global semiconductor market. Can you cut off your own companies and those of your friends and allies from 40 per cent of a market without doing them serious damage? This impels a policy of fine judgements rather than a simple decision to cut supplies. In 2022, the *Wall Street Journal* reported that most applications for exemptions to Biden-era bans on exports of technology to China had been approved.[28] More restrictions on the transfer of semiconductors and other high technologies have since been passed and more are probably in the pipeline. But it is unlikely any legislation can entirely reshape the realities of complex competition. Like water, if blocked in one direction, trade flows will find other channels to reach where they must.

The geopolitical implications of the new world economy are profound. China does not pose an existential threat to the United States. In fact, after the collapse of the Soviet Union, the United States faces no existential threat anywhere in the world. Vladimir Putin's Russia is certainly dangerous and undoubtedly an existential threat to Ukraine, and perhaps also to the Baltic states and some of the countries that used to form its bloc in Eastern Europe. But is Russia an existential threat to the United States? I don't think so. Similarly, other states that the United States considers 'rogue' – Iran and North Korea – may pose existential threats to other states in their regions, but not to the United States.

Facing no existential threat anywhere in the world, there is no longer any compelling reason for the United States, in the words of John F. Kennedy at the height of the Cold War, to 'pay any price, bear any burden, meet any hardship, support any friend, oppose any foe to assure the survival and success of liberty'.[29] That ideal of American global leadership developed in response to a world that no longer exists and is never going to return.

It is no longer tenable for any post-Cold War president to exhort Americans to 'ask not what your country can do for you – ask what you can do for your country'. It is now eminently reasonable for Americans to instead ask what their country could at long last do for them, particularly those Americans neglected and left behind in the immediate post-Cold War decades of hyper-globalisation. After 40 years of international engagement during the Cold War, often at great sacrifice of American blood and treasure, it is time to put 'America First'. The foremost priorities of every post-Cold War president have been domestic, with George W. Bush as an exception forced by 9/11. So Donald Trump is not sui generis. He is different only in the extent to which he has taken the idea, and the extreme rhetoric in which he expresses it. Trump may be a catalyst speeding up the changes in US foreign policy, but he did not initiate them.

However, putting 'America First' is not, as some commentators have represented it, isolationism or a retreat from the world. There is nothing unusual about a country putting its own interests first. That is a fundamental operating principle of all diplomacy for all countries. Putting your own interest first does not mean withdrawing from the world. Trump's comments on buying Greenland, annexing the Panama Canal, taking over Gaza, and making Canada the 51st state, regardless of whether he means it or not, are the very opposite of isolationism.

Trump is not a free-trader. Free-traders are rare in contemporary America. Apart from that short, exceptional, immediate post-Cold War period, free trade has always been politically contentious in the United States, and many antecedents that share Trump's attitudes can be identified in the history of American controversies over trade.[30] Trump is not against trade per se. He is not seeking autarky. Trump is against what he regards as unfair trade, which, unfortunately for the rest of us, in his view means any trade that results in a trade deficit for America. In his first term, he renounced the Trans-Pacific Partnership, which was not yet in force. But he renegotiated the North

American Free Trade Agreement and the US-Korea Free Trade Agreement to get better deals for the United States.

That said, Trump's use of tariffs on a scale not seen for decades risks taking us from 'known unknowns' into the territory of 'unknown unknowns'. The key factor here is US-China relations, and the risk that trade tensions will escalate geopolitical tensions. Still, there are glimmers of hope to believe that the worst outcomes can be avoided. China has retaliated, as was only to be expected. Yet Beijing has also signalled that although it will not negotiate under duress, it is prepared to come to a deal. Trump also wants a deal. The current state of US-China relations is like two enormous MMA fighters who have entered the ring and are standing there snarling, spitting, and hurling insults at each other, but do not really want to rush to come to grips because they know both will get hurt. But neither yet knows how to back down without looking weak, and, of course, even the saliva of such behemoths can hurt bystanders.

For US allies, partners, and friends, putting 'America First' represents a narrower and more transactional definition of American national interests and creates the expectation that they should do more for themselves and compensate America more for what it does for them. The United States will calculate its national interests carefully before it decides whether and how to get involved internationally, and in many cases it may decide not to get involved or only involve itself for the time necessary to deal with a particular situation.

This too is not new, although it may appear so if we focus only on the immediate. In 1796, in his farewell address, President George Washington warned against permanent alliances. Before the Second World War, the United States engaged in external affairs only episodically. It took a direct attack on Pearl Harbor in 1941 to force the United States to confront the threats posed by fascism in Europe and militarism in Japan; after 1945 it was the existential threat of the Soviet Union that led the United States into the Cold War. The 50 years between Pearl Harbor and the implosion of the Soviet Union in 1991 was the longest period of sustained external engagement in 250 years of American history, only about 20 per cent of its existence.

Trump's decision to try to end the fighting in Ukraine, even at Kyiv's expense, was a severe shock to Europe. But this too is not without precedent in US foreign policy. The big shift in the US approach towards East Asia did not occur when Trump was first elected in 2016 but almost half a century earlier. In

1969, as part of the process of disengaging the United States from an unwinnable war in Vietnam, Richard Nixon announced the 'Guam Doctrine' under which the United States would maintain overall nuclear deterrence but eschew ground interventions in Asia. The United States expected its allies, partners, and friends in East Asia to take more responsibility for their own defence, while America acted as offshore balancer to maintain overall stability through its forces based in Okinawa and Yokosuka in Japan and on its Pacific territory of Guam.

In 1973, the United States withdrew from mainland Southeast Asia, abandoning South Vietnam, Laos, and Cambodia to their fates. Although Nixon had signalled his intentions four years earlier in his Guam speech, it was nevertheless a shock to America's Asian allies, partners, and friends, similar to the shock Europe is reeling from today because of Trump's attempt to force a stop to the Ukraine war. It should be no surprise that, unlike Europe, most Asian countries have taken their own defence seriously for decades. When China turned more assertive after Xi Jinping took power in 2012, Asia was building on a solid base. The International Institute for Strategic Studies estimates that since 2014, defence budgets in Asia, excluding China, have grown by an average of three per cent annually.[31]

If Asians have not been complacent about defence, it is perhaps because in East Asia, the United States only has firm treaty obligations to defend Japan and South Korea. US treaties with Australia, the Philippines, and Thailand only oblige the United States to 'consult' with these countries and act 'in accordance with its constitutional process' if they are threatened. In other words, if the United States defends these countries, it will be the result of a political decision, and such decisions are always contingent on circumstances. Since the mid-1980s, the United States no longer has even this minimal obligation to New Zealand after it refused to let US naval ships visit its ports unless they confirmed they were not carrying nuclear weapons.

The allies, partners, and friends of an offshore balancer are always going to be anxious about its commitment: an offshore balancer will arouse fears of entanglement if it acts robustly, and fears of abandonment if it decides not to get involved or only minimally involved. The porridge is always going to be regarded as too hot by some and too cold by others and seldom, if ever, just right by everyone. Concerns about US reliability have been endemic in Asia for decades. Still, despite inevitable gyrations of policy from different administrations, the United States has been remarkably consistent for almost half a century in maintaining equilibrium in Asia as an offshore balancer.

Since there is no substitute for the United States, whether it is reliable or not is moot. Asia works with the United States because it must, but it has not used the United States in the way Europe did, as a crutch. Recently, I heard a former European prime minister, speaking at a conference in an Asian country, repeat three times, in the tones of a jilted lover, that all his life he had taken US support for granted but now he, like the rest of Europe, had to reassess his beliefs. The poor fellow was palpably, utterly discombobulated. Yet since the end of the Cold War, every American president has called on Europe to take its own defence more seriously but could not get their attention until Trump became president in 2017. When Joe Biden replaced Trump four years later, most Europeans again happily lost themselves in a fantasy in which American support was unconditional and they could indefinitely free-ride on America for security.

This is not a fantasy that, after the Vietnam War, any Asian country ever found beguiling, with Australia as a possible and partial exception. I doubt any Asian country has forgotten the fate of the Indochinese governments that put their unqualified faith in the United States to defend them. In April

1975, as Khmer Rouge forces closed in on Phnom Penh, US Ambassador John Gunther Dean wrote to senior members of the Cambodian government, offering them asylum in the United States. One senior Cambodian, Prince Sisowath Sirik Matak, wrote to Dean to thank him for the offer to 'transport me towards freedom', but that he could not leave in 'such a cowardly fashion . . . if I shall die here on the spot and in my country that I love, it is too bad, because we are all born and must die one day. I have only committed this mistake of believing in you, the Americans.'[32] Sirik Matak and perhaps as many as two million more Cambodians were murdered by the Khmer Rouge. The fates of those left behind in Laos and South Vietnam were not as horrific but bad enough.

Most Asian countries, including US treaty allies, partners, and friends (again with Australia as an exception) have dealt with the United States more on the basis of common interests than the illusion of common values. A persistent theme in the writings of the American theologian and philosopher Reinhold Niebuhr is that the most significant characteristic of all nations is hypocrisy and that Americans, being uncomfortable with power, have felt the need to wrap up their interests in ideas of wider moral significance when deploying power in pursuit of those interests.[33] But at least since the ignominious end to US involvement in the Indochina wars, most Asian governments have not mistaken the theology of American foreign policy for American interests.

The end of the Cold War marked a profound structural change in international relations. It is therefore entirely natural that this has initiated change in American priorities and how America engages with the world. The shift to domestic priorities and changes in the terms of America's global engagement will persist in some degree and form regardless of who occupies the White House.

From this perspective, Donald Trump and his predecessors are more alike than any of them would be comfortable admitting. Bill Clinton's focus was on health care. When Barack Obama talked about 'change', he was not talking primarily about change abroad but change at home. Is there a very great difference between Trump wanting to 'Make America Great Again' and Biden wanting to 'Build Back Better'? Internationally, Biden was solicitous about consulting allies, partners, and friends, and that is an important difference. But Biden was not consulting us to enquire how our families were doing; he was consulting us to see what we were prepared to do to advance American interests. Call it polite transactionalism.

Where Trump differs sharply is in his belief that America is strong enough not to have to be polite about what it wants. Trump has ripped the moralistic wrapping off American foreign policy and exposed certain eternal verities. He sees no reason to appeal to any higher principle than putting America First. An America that puts itself first wants to maintain primacy without admitting any responsibilities except those dictated by its interests.

Still, pre-Trump America was not some prelapsarian paradise. The City on the Hill has always cast dark shadows, a fact that has been more evident to those who live below the hill than on it. Unilateralism, distrust of multilateral institutions, emphasising strength, and the making of threats, were not invented by Donald Trump. He obviously does not believe in speaking softly, but belongs to a venerable American diplomatic tradition of brandishing a big stick. His methods may be raw, but they are working – so far.

As I write this in July 2025, the big stick has worked in Panama, Columbia, and Venezuela, and the responses of Canada, Mexico, and Denmark to Trump's outlandish threats have been relatively muted. Taiwanese and South Korean companies have pledged substantial investments in the United States, and others will follow.[34] Other countries are considering reducing their own tariffs and what they can buy from America to mitigate the effects of Trump's tariffs. After talks in Geneva in May, the United States and China agreed to de-escalate their trade war.

The United States is still the world's largest and most innovative economy, possessing the world's most technologically sophisticated military with unmatched war-fighting experience. China's military hardware is growing quantitatively, but its ability to use it effectively against the United States is still an open question. The People's Liberation Army (PLA) has not fought a war since its 1979 conflict with Vietnam, and while its sheer weight ultimately prevailed, that was a Pyrrhic victory with perhaps more than 20,000 Chinese soldiers killed in one month of fighting. Europe is incapable of dealing with Russia without US backing. As for Asia, even if it could act collectively, Japan, South Korea, India, Australia, and the ASEAN countries cannot balance China by themselves.

Countries may wring their hands, gnash their teeth, and rend their garments, they will squirm and grumble, but ultimately they must recognise that there is no alternative to the United States either in economic or strategic terms. Countries may hedge by diversifying their relationships, but there is only one America and no one has any choice but to deal with it no matter how the administration of the day may behave. Most Asian countries will find a way of doing so.

Approaching the United States on the basis of common interests, as Asia has done for decades, fits neatly into Trump's transactional approach and his penchant for making deals. The key question for Asia is: what kind of deal will Trump make with China?

That he will try to cut some sort of deal is a given. Deal-making is in the marrow of his bones, and he believes no one is better at it than himself. Trump is not ideologically anti-China, but China is his target whether the goal is to maintain American primacy, reduce the trade deficit, force a reorientation of supply chains to bring manufacturing back to America, or stop the flow of fentanyl to the United States.

There is a theory that Trump favours Russian interests in Ukraine because he wants to pry Moscow and Beijing apart in a reverse Nixon-Kissinger strategy. This is unpersuasive. I doubt Moscow and Beijing will split. Neither country has any partner of comparable strategic weight anywhere in the world that shares their distrust of the West. Beijing and Moscow must hang together lest they hang separately. The Trump administration's initial moves on Ukraine seem to have made Xi Jinping feel it necessary to reassure Putin that China and Russia are 'true friends who share weal and woe, support each other and develop together'.[35] It was in Xi's interest to say this and in Putin's interest to believe him.

An alternative theory is that Trump admires strongman leaders such as Putin and Xi, and wants a Yalta-like 'grand bargain' with Russia and China involving not just trade but geopolitical issues and the division of the world into spheres of influence. This is improbable. Such a deal would leave most of Asia in the Chinese sphere of influence. Much as Trump relishes deal-making, he is even more interested in winning and being seen to win. A 'grand bargain' that concedes the fastest-growing region of the world to China will be seen as a clear loss for America. Trump will not want to go down in history as a loser who was bamboozled by China.

One theory assumes that the United States wants to divide Russia from China, while the other assumes that the United States wants to work with both Russia and China. I prefer to apply Occam's Razor: the most straightforward reason why Trump wants to force an end to the fighting in Ukraine is to concentrate on China. The Ukraine war is a second-order issue.

Days before the end of the first Trump administration, it declassified and released a lightly redacted cabinet memo entitled 'US Strategic Framework for the Indo-Pacific'. The Biden administration's own Indo-Pacific strategy paper released in February 2022 was very similar. During his four years as president, Biden's approach towards key issues such as China and trade largely built upon and extended policies initiated by Trump.[36]

This does not mean Trump 2.0 will be identical to Biden and Trump 1.0. But several of the second Trump administration's early moves could be seen as setting the stage for long-term strategic competition with China. The acquisition by a BlackRock-led consortium of Hong Kong-based Hutchison's stake in 43 ports across 23 countries is of particular significance because it kicks a gaping hole in China's logistics network, giving an American company control over about a third of it. Xi Jinping is reportedly angry over the deal, suggesting that he too sees it as strategically disadvantaging China.[37] Regardless of whether they succeed or fail, attempts to bring manufacturing back to the United States and Trump's interest in acquiring control over minerals in Ukraine, Greenland, and Canada are also indicative of preparations for long-term strategic competition with China.

It is still early days for the second Trump administration. But these moves, plus Defence Secretary Pete Hegseth's March 2025 tour of Asia, at very least do not suggest Trump intends to meekly surrender the field to China. In his inaugural speech at the Shangri-La Dialogue in Singapore in May 2025, Hegseth delivered a strong, clear message: 'The United States is an Indo-Pacific nation . . . since the earliest days of our Republic . . . We will not be pushed out of this critical region'.[38]

We must separate Trump's tactics and extravagant rhetoric from his intent. Fears of America being fooled into conceding too much to China or Russia often reflect distaste for Trump's personality and condescension about his mental capabilities by the elites he has marginalised. Trump is no intellectual but he is very far from being a fool. His instinct for exercising hard power should not be underestimated. For example, in his first term, Trump dealt with North Korea much better than his predecessor, restoring deterrence lost by Obama, who made pretty speeches but came across in Asia as weak, including to US treaty allies.[39]

Making deals with China does not mean an end to competition with China. Rather than a 'grand bargain', it is more likely Trump will cut narrower deals on trade, portraying them as huge wins, while continuing to press China in other domains. The second Trump administration has added to the restrictions on technology exports to China put in place by the Biden administration. Trump's deals will certainly always put 'America First', but we should not assume that they will necessarily be bad for other Asian countries.

This is not to say that there are no risks. A dynamic of tit-for-tat tariffs between the United States, China, and other major economies will accentuate the economic challenges facing Beijing and may tip the world into a recession. Even if that is avoided, the well-trodden export-led growth path that brought Japan, Taiwan, South Korea, and Singapore to high-income status will almost certainly become much rockier and steeper for others, including those parts of China that are still relatively undeveloped. Some countries and regions may fall into the middle-income trap, while others may not escape low income. Such divisions could exacerbate existing geopolitical fault lines in Asia. Rather than dealing with a rising China, we may have to deal with a frustrated China, which could be more challenging.

Amidst the flux and clamour of American politics, continuity is more often to be found in themes unfolding over the long term than in the policies of particular administrations. In *By More Than*

Providence, Michael Green describes the unifying thread of America's grand strategy in the region thus: 'The United States will not tolerate *any other power* establishing exclusive hegemonic control over Asia or the Pacific.' [emphasis added][40]

The idea that American interests should be given special preference – put first – existed long before Trump turned it into a powerful political slogan. The disruptions in Trump's Asia policies are more in his methods than his goals. There is a strong presumption that these disruptions must rebound to China's benefit in Asia. This is simplistic. Most Asian countries do not see the world in such binary terms, and while China is influential, it is not trusted. It is to China and the complexities of Asian attitudes towards China that we now turn.

CHAPTER FOUR

Has China already lost?

By virtue of its size, its contiguity, its economic weight, and its crucial role in the world economy, China will always enjoy considerable influence in Asia, particularly Southeast Asia. But for those same reasons, China will always arouse anxieties in Asia and indeed the world. Deng Xiaoping's approach of hiding China's power and biding time stems from his awareness of this paradox. Big countries need to reassure small countries on their periphery. Deng recognised this and acted on it.

But by the end of the Hu Jintao era, Deng's wisdom was either forgotten or ignored, perhaps because Beijing over-read the implications of the 2008 global financial crisis and, just as the United States had done with the end of the Cold War, invested it with a universal significance as heralding

Marx's long-predicted decline and eventual collapse of the West, specifically the United States.

In July 2010, at an ASEAN-sponsored meeting in Hanoi, then Chinese Foreign Minister Yang Jiechi imperiously proclaimed: 'China is a big country and other countries are small countries, and that's just a fact.' Yang was reported to have been looking at the Singapore foreign minister when he issued this warning because Singapore had been audacious enough to defy Chinese wishes by talking about the South China Sea. But all other ASEAN members were present at the meeting and several of them had raised the issue before Yang's outburst.[41]

In September 2005, Zheng Bijian, an influential intellectual and senior adviser to the Chinese government, had published an article in the American journal *Foreign Affairs* entitled 'China's "Peaceful Rise" to Great-Power Status'.[42] This became the dominant theme in Chinese foreign policy discourse, though 'rise' was later deemed too provocative and replaced by 'development'. China recognised that falling out with the United States and its allies could derail China's growth.

But after Xi Jinping took power in 2012, 'peaceful development' faded from the Chinese foreign policy lexicon. Instead, the dominant note was struck by the slogan 'the East rising and the West declining', which resonated with Politburo Standing Committee member Wang Huning's *America Against America*, an account of his six-month visit to the United States in 1988. It is a catalogue of America's failings, not all inaccurate, but one-sided and superficial in its portrayal of the United States.[43]

China became more aggressive after Xi took power, not just in the South China Sea but against Hong Kong, in the East China Sea, around Taiwan and Australia, and in the Himalayas. This has raised anxiety levels across Asia. It does not, however, follow that Asia will meekly submit to China's wishes. Singapore and other ASEAN members have continued to discuss the South China Sea in ASEAN forums. The United States has continued to conduct regular freedom of navigation operations in the South China Sea. Japan, Australia, and India have conducted naval patrols. The United Kingdom, France, and Germany, among other European countries, have also occasionally sent their naval vessels to the South China Sea, investing the issue with an international dimension that Beijing had tried to avoid.

An important but inadequately recognised development over the last 30 years or so has been an unarticulated but perceptible shift of attitude towards the US military presence in Southeast Asia in response to anxieties about China. Diplomatic partnerships such as the Quad (between Australia, India, Japan, and the United States), security agreements such as AUKUS (the Australia-UK-US partnership to supply Australia with nuclear-powered submarines and co-develop other exotic military technologies), Japan's increase in defence spending and more proactive external posture, and India's abandonment of purist interpretations of non-alignment, are all responses to China, and have attracted more attention. But what has quietly occurred in Southeast Asia is not without consequence either.

Singapore has, since independence, not been shy about making known its view that the US role in maintaining balance across East Asia was irreplaceable. British military bases in Singapore – part of the global American network – nearly scuttled the formation of ASEAN when Indonesia, supported by Malaysia, insisted on their removal. But so vital was this point to Singapore that its first Foreign Minister, S. Rajaratnam, was prepared to walk out of the 1967 meeting in Bangkok that was drafting the declaration that set up ASEAN. The Thai Foreign Minister, Thanat Khoman, persuaded him to stay and an eleventh-hour compromise was found.

In 1988, the United States and the Philippines began negotiations on the extension of the agreement that allowed the US military to station forces in Subic Bay and Clark Air Base. The negotiations quickly ran into difficulties. The proximate cause was leasing costs but the real issue was the strong anti-American streak in Filipino nationalism, which became more prominent after Ferdinand Marcos fell from power in 1986. In June 1991, a volcanic eruption buried both bases under ash and brought matters to a head. Clark Air Base was declared a total loss. Subic was quickly cleaned up, but the refusal of the Philippine Senate to ratify the renewal agreement in September of that year killed it. By November 1992, the last US sailors and marines left Subic and the American flag was lowered after almost a hundred years, a victim of Filipino politics and a natural disaster.

As the negotiations floundered and it became increasingly obvious that they would fail, Singapore decided to put its money where its mouth had long been and offered the US military the use of some of its facilities. It was by no stretch an adequate substitute for Subic Bay – drop Singapore Island into the bay and we will never be found again. But Singapore thought that even a symbolic US military presence in Southeast Asia was better than none and acted accordingly. In 1990, a Memorandum of Understanding (MOU) was signed between the United States and Singapore to put this into effect.

All hell broke loose. Indonesia and Malaysia reacted hysterically, as if Singapore were conspiring with the devil to sell their children into slavery. Immense pressure was put on Singapore by its closest neighbours to rescind the MOU. Of course, Singapore did no such thing. Fast forward to 2019 when the 1990 MOU was renewed with full publicity at a signing ceremony between the Singapore Prime Minister and President Trump, held at the United Nations in New York. What happened? The answer is 'nothing'. Nothing happened. There was not a whimper of protest.

Nor was there any criticism from any ASEAN country in 2005 when Singapore and the United States concluded a Strategic Framework Agreement that raised their defence cooperation significantly higher than that of America's formal Southeast Asian treaty allies, Thailand and the Philippines. I wish I could claim the change in the responses of our neighbours between 1990 and 2019 as a brilliant success for Singapore diplomacy. But in truth it was much more due to the failures of Chinese diplomacy. While attitudes towards China and the United States vary from country to country and, as will be explained later in this chapter, are in any case complex, rising anxieties about China now makes what Singapore does to anchor a US military presence in

Southeast Asia something of a regional public good. Our immediate neighbours in particular will never acknowledge it as such, but this has more to do with their attitude towards Singapore than to the United States.

Domestic politics sometimes places constraints on what ASEAN members can do with the United States or are willing to admit doing. Nevertheless, several ASEAN members have been quietly expanding defence ties through participation in military exercises with the United States and its allies, port calls by US naval vessels, and procurement of American military equipment. What Vietnam, which fought a bitter war with the United States and still has more than 200,000 soldiers missing, and Indonesia, with its strong tradition of a '*Bebas dan Aktif*' (free and active) policy of non-alignment, are doing is particularly telling.[44]

Why are these shifts of attitude insufficiently recognised? From the 20th century to the present, Americans have often conceptualised Asia in binary and universalistic terms: as contests between communist oppression and Western freedom or where tides of dictatorship and democracy ebb and flow. Policy was too often conceived of as a Manichean struggle – as if any advance by the states personifying one of these abstractions was a retreat from the other.

Today, anything an Asian, and especially Southeast Asian, country does with China is often seen as at least a potential concern for the United States. China has a parallel attitude, displayed in Xi Jinping's emphasis on the slogan 'the East rising and the West declining', its insistence that Asian problems should be solved by Asians, and in the over-used trope of the American century being replaced by an Asian century.

Asia is one of the most diverse continents, consisting of 48 countries with a population of 4.6 billion speaking approximately 2,300 languages, and Southeast Asia is one of its most diverse subregions, consisting of ten states with a population of about 700 million speaking more than a thousand languages. Reducing this complexity to a kind of geopolitical Rorschach test that betrays your deepest fears or hopes, or reducing it to a blank sheet on which abstract universals or simplistic binaries are projected and play out, is analytically unsound but, unfortunately, all too common. One could call it the Binary Trap.

In September 2024, Lynn Kuok, the Lee Kuan Yew Chair in Southeast Asia Studies at the Brookings Institution, published an article in *Foreign Affairs* entitled 'America is Losing Southeast Asia: Why US Allies in the Region are Turning toward China'.[45]

Dr Kuok's conclusion, encapsulated in the title, is an example of a broad category of commentary that falls into this binary trap.

Kuok drew her conclusion essentially from just one question in the 2024 edition of Singapore's Yusof Ishak Institute of Southeast Asian Studies (ISEAS) annual *State of Southeast Asia* survey. A range of regional experts and opinion leaders are polled for the survey, which consists of more than 60 questions covering an array of topics. Question 32 was phrased as follows: 'If ASEAN were forced to align itself with one of the strategic rivals [United States or China], which should it choose?'. For the first time, the majority picked China over the United States. However, the margin was paper thin – 50.5 per cent for China to 49.5 per cent for the United States.[46] The 2025 survey reversed the finding of the 2024 survey with 52.3 per cent for the United States and 47.7 per cent for China, a larger margin.[47] This is a slender reed to support the weight of the conclusion that 'America is losing Southeast Asia', so requires explanation.

After Trump was elected for a second time, intellectual elites around the world – not all American or European, but who had attended the same universities as Western elites, spoke the same languages, read many of the same books and journals, and thus had absorbed some of their values – were stunned and profoundly dismayed to find that the President of the United States and the Americans who had twice voted him into office did not share values they had been accustomed to think of as the natural order of things.

Their shock led many to seek, probably unconsciously, psychological consolation by regarding Trump's every move as wrong or backfiring to China's advantage. This is the underlying theme of much commentary since the second Trump administration began what these elites regard as its blitzkrieg against the existing order.

The starkly binary manner in which ISEAS posed its question was misleading. The next question was more open-ended, asking which third parties ASEAN should look to in order to hedge against the uncertainties of US-China rivalry. The results were evenly distributed, with the European Union and Japan coming out on top with 37.2 per cent and 27.7 per cent respectively, and Australia, India, and the United Kingdom running more or less even with 9.5 per cent, 10.5 per cent, and 9.2 per cent respectively. South Korea trailed behind with 5.9 per cent.

ISEAS has conducted these surveys since 2019, and on examination of the series, a far more complex and accurate picture of Southeast Asian attitudes towards major and middle powers emerges. The ISEAS surveys have consistently shown that, while China is widely recognised as very influential, Beijing is also widely and deeply mistrusted. American intellectuals, who are sometimes overly self-critical, may be surprised to learn that the 2024 survey showed that 42.4 per cent of respondents were confident or very confident that the United States would do the 'right thing' to contribute to global peace, security, prosperity, and governance. The comparable number for China was only 24.8 per cent. America's principal regional ally, Japan, has consistently been the most trusted external power.[48]

All opinion surveys must be used with caution. But what the ISEAS surveys show, when taken in totality, is the complexity of Southeast Asian attitudes towards external powers. None is entirely trusted, although some are more trusted than others. They are trusted or distrusted for different reasons in different domains. It is futile to try to force attitudes into any consistent pattern.

For instance, despite the official caution of most ASEAN governments towards the Quad, the ISEAS survey showed that in 2023 slightly more than half (50.4 per cent) of those surveyed agreed or strongly agreed that strengthening the Quad was positive and reassuring for Southeast Asia. In 2024, 40.9 per cent believed cooperation with the Quad would be beneficial to the region and 32.2 per cent thought it could complement ASEAN's own efforts. Only minorities of those surveyed thought the Quad would provoke China (7.4 per cent), force ASEAN to choose sides (7.9 per cent), or threaten ASEAN's centrality (11.5 per cent).

Yet this positive attitude towards the Quad does not equate to confidence in the United States, which has dropped with only about 35 per cent considering the United States a reliable security partner in 2024 compared to slightly more than 47 per cent in 2023.[49] But if you really think the United States is unreliable, why improve defence ties with it or think the Quad, which has the United States at its centre, is not a bad thing?

In Asian diplomacy, consistency is not necessarily a virtue. To adapt a saying attributed to the great American novelist F. Scott Fitzgerald, most Asians have absolutely no difficulty in holding two or more opposing ideas in our minds at the same time while still retaining the ability to function. That is how our diplomacy usually works. In this respect, Fitzgerald's quip provides deeper insights into Asian statecraft than do many political scientists and experts on the region (although there are notable exceptions).[50] Asia is a messy place, and a frame of mind that seeks to impose orderly answers on disorderly reality can lead to dubious conclusions. Better to embrace the contradictions.

This often baffles outsiders, particularly when we say 'we do not want to choose' between the United States and China. The phrase is more frequently used than understood. I shall attempt to explain with reference to my own country, Singapore.

When we say 'we do not want to choose', we do *not* mean we want to be 'neutral', because neutrality is a status that has to be accepted and respected by other parties and we have no confidence they will do so. We do *not* mean that we want to be 'equidistant' between the United States and China, because we are not sure what that means and even if we were to find out, we are uncertain that it is even possible. And we certainly do *not* mean lying low, staying mum, and hoping to be left alone, because Southeast Asian history in the second half of the 20th century has provided tragic examples of countries that tried to do just that.

What we mean is that we intend to exercise our sovereignty to choose according to our own national interests as we determine them. How we define our interests will vary from domain to domain. We see no need to neatly line up all our interests across all domains in one direction or another.

In the defence and security domain, Singapore long ago clearly chose the United States and the West generally. But on some political matters – for example, the claim that the so-called universality of certain political ideas and rights gives countries a voice in how we in Singapore manage our internal affairs – our attitudes are closer to those of China or Russia, which sometimes disconcerts the United States and other Western partners. And in economic relations, we are positively promiscuous and will negotiate with whoever offers a deal that is in accordance with our interests, prudence, and law.

I have used my own country as an example of what in various degrees and in different ways, according to national circumstances, is a general Asian attitude towards diplomacy. This attitude is the consequence of a regional environment that more often than not throughout modern history has been shaped by geopolitics and major-power rivalry of which US-China rivalry is only the latest iteration. To most of Asia, dealing with great-power competition is a normal state of affairs, and hedging, balancing, and bandwagoning are not alternative strategies, as they are usually presented in Western international relations theory. Most Asians see no contradiction in simultaneously hedging, balancing, and bandwagoning in different domains vis-à-vis different external powers.

I do not claim that Asia always plays this game well, but in principle this is what Asia usually tries to do.

Asian, particularly Southeast Asian, diplomacy has almost always been polygamous or omnidirectional. This is true even of US treaty allies, again with the possible and partial exception of Australia, which is perhaps why Australians seem to feel more keenly betrayed than America's other Asian allies now that their true love no longer feels obliged to reciprocate their feelings. Other Asian allies, such as Japan, have not forgotten the 'shocks' America administered to them, such as Nixon's visit to China in 1972, overturning a decades-old approach without informing any ally, or the 1985 Plaza Accord that precipitated a decade of slow growth. Their relationship with the United States, while close, has never been a starry-eyed love affair.

Underlying this omnidirectional diplomacy is what I earlier identified as the most powerful force in Asia: nationalism. Nationalism overcame colonialism; it often frustrated the designs of the Soviet Union, China, the United States, and Europe. With only two tragic exceptions – Laos and Cambodia – nationalism helped Southeast Asia navigate the dangers of the Cold War.

Nationalism underscores an important but under-analysed fact of international relations: even the smallest state in the most dire of circumstances always has agency. There is always something they can do. This is an intrinsic condition of international relations and if it were not so, Singapore would not exist as an independent and sovereign state and neither would many others. Of course, whether or not those states have the wit to recognise the opportunities to exercise agency and the courage and skill to use them are different matters. Mistakes occur, and examining the mistakes made by the two tragic exceptions I mentioned – Laos and Cambodia – is instructive.

Confronted with the spill-over effects of the war in Vietnam, Laos and Cambodia both first adopted an essentially passive form of neutrality – lying low and hoping for the best – and when this did not work, they joined South Vietnam in placing their fate in the hands of an external patron, the United States. Both approaches surrendered agency to others, with the consequences we now know. Today, these two countries seem on the verge of repeating their mistake with China as their new patron, Laos much more than Cambodia. But I doubt any other Asian country will again so totally surrender agency to any external power. That is why talking of America or China or any other country having 'lost' or 'won' a country or region is condescending nonsense: the countries that make up Asia were never anyone's to 'lose' or 'win' in the first place.

A particularly egregious version of this attitude is the assumption made by more simple-minded commentators that because China is the biggest, or among the biggest, trading partner of all Asian countries, Beijing will call the shots. This is an insulting and ethnocentric attitude as it assumes that we 'natives' are so venal as to sell our national interests for a mess of pottage or so stupid as not to know our own interests in the first place. It is also a gross simplification of how states make decisions and define their interests. Not every strategic calculation can be reduced to trade or economics.

In 2024, trade between the ten ASEAN states and China amounted to US$982 billion; the figure for ASEAN and the United States was just under US$477 billion. But if you factor in ASEAN's trade with American allies – the European Union (US$279.9 billion), Japan (US$239.5 billion), South Korea (US$196.9 billion), and Australia (US$192.9 billion) – ASEAN's trade with the West as a whole is in excess of US$1 trillion. These figures are for 2023, but they clearly show that Southeast Asia's overall economic orientation is not unduly skewed towards China.

How patterns of trade will change during the second Trump administration is yet to be seen. What is already clear is that Beijing relies too much on its economic weight as a diplomatic tool, and Chinese diplomats and scholars sometimes appear somewhat puzzled and frustrated when trade, investment, and aid, not to mention what can be euphemistically called 'informal payments', do not win trust for China. I have had occasion to remind some of my Chinese friends that even the most corrupt individual can be a nationalist. Beijing's attempts at economic coercion have not changed basic strategic directions: not in Japan, South Korea, or Australia, and not even in a weak and corrupt country like the Philippines.

Every country must deal with China. No country will ever shun China. Every country wants as good a relationship with China as possible. But China's overall geopolitical situation is not favourable.

Which countries in the vast arc of countries from Northeast Asia, down through Southeast Asia, and into South Asia, trust China or will meekly acquiesce to China occupying the apex of a regional hierarchy?

Despite having absorbed much of Chinese culture, the core identities of Japan, North and South Korea, and Vietnam have for centuries been defined in opposition to China and the Sinosphere. They cannot subordinate themselves to China without such a wrenching redefinition of identity as to make every other alternative less painful.

Under the late Prime Minister Abe Shinzo, Japan finally broke with the post-war Yoshida Doctrine that voluntarily subordinated Japan's security role to the United States so that Japan could concentrate on economic development. Abe passed legislation that circumvented constitutional restraints on Japanese defence policies and under his leadership, Japan began to play a more proactive external role. Weak post-Abe political leaders will slow this process, but the direction will not change because these are responses to permanent changes in Japan's strategic environment.[51]

In Southeast Asia, Indonesia is a strongly nationalist country that since independence has followed its own path despite attempts by the Soviet Union, Maoist China, Cold War America, and Europe to capture it. Vietnam is strongly nationalist, too. It is impossible for any external power to capture Southeast Asia without first bringing these two countries under its sway.

India is as ancient and populous a country as China and will never accept a subaltern status to it. The energies of such a vast, complicated, and rambunctious country as India will always be primarily internally focused, but it has already begun to play a greater external role.[52] China's ability to use Europe to hedge against uncertainties in its relations with the United States will be limited unless Beijing breaks with Moscow, and Europe can have no real strategic autonomy to work with China so long as it remains incapable of deterring Russia without the United States at its back. Even in countries highly dependent on China, such as Pakistan, Laos, and Cambodia, ground-level attitudes towards Beijing are often at variance with those of their governments.

China's reputation is better in the Global South. But that term invests the motley group of countries it refers to with undue coherence. The Global South represents only a mood (grievances about colonial history and its effects on development, and a desire for a stronger international voice), not any real convergence of interests. The institutions that profess to represent this mood – the Non-Aligned Movement, the G77, and its latest manifestation, BRICS (a multilateral group named after Brazil, Russia, India, China, and South Africa, but which now includes five other developing country members, with others set to join) – are rent with internal conflicts of interests that make their ability to act in unison largely performative. India, a key member of BRICS, clearly mistrusts China. Egypt, another key member, is dependent on Western economic and military aid. Of the BRICS group, only Russia and Iran share China's anti-Western streak.

China is aware of its poor reputation. From the first year he took power, Xi Jinping emphasised the need for 'telling China's story well', and has repeatedly used the slogan. In June 2021, in the face of growing international criticism of its 'wolf warrior diplomacy', Xi told senior CCP officials that it was important to present an image of a 'credible, lovable, and respectable China'.[53]

The harshest tones of its 'wolf warrior diplomacy' have since been moderated, but not its substance. There has been no change in Chinese behaviour in the East and South China Seas, towards Taiwan, and in the Himalayas. Beijing seems to believe its own propaganda about the decline of the West and it has prematurely abandoned Deng Xiaoping's approach of hiding capabilities and biding time. Some brave Chinese intellectuals have warned about the dangers of underestimating America or thinking it is in absolute decline.[54] There is no sign that Xi has taken any notice. If anything, China's actions have become more aggressive on his watch.

Why is it so difficult for Beijing to stop or even substantively modify counterproductive behaviour? First of all, it may regard the reputational damage as a sunk cost because it is convinced – not entirely without cause – that the West, and particularly the United States, is set on containing China and stymieing its growth no matter what China does. Moreover, once you have revealed your intentions by your actions, they are not going to be easily forgotten by others. I doubt Beijing really believes that piously claiming that its foreign policy is motivated by the desire for a 'community of common destiny for mankind' is going to cut any ice except with the terminally gullible. Whatever you may think of them, China's leaders cannot be accused of naivety.

But there is a more fundamental reason why Beijing cannot modify its behaviour. On 11 November 2021, the Sixth Plenary Session of the 19th Central Committee of the Chinese Communist Party adopted a resolution on the 'Major Achievements and Historical Experience of the Party over the Last Century'. The resolution melded China's dynastic tradition with Marxist dialectical materialism. In this retelling of Chinese history, the revolutions of 1911 and 1949 are only superficial ruptures with the past. More essentially, they are presented as stages in an unbroken historical process whose inevitable culmination will be the CCP's realisation of the China Dream under its leadership. This conception of Chinese history is the foundation that supports the CCP's legitimating ethno-nationalist narrative of China's humiliation, rejuvenation, and eventual realisation of the China Dream.

The importance of this narrative to the CCP cannot be overstated. No government can rule by coercion alone. Since the end of the Qing Dynasty, the legitimacy of every Chinese government has rested on its ability to protect China's sovereignty and territorial integrity. Xi has emphasised the narrative of humiliation, rejuvenation, and achieving the China Dream more insistently than any of his predecessors. The resolution on history – only the second ever adopted by the CCP – was his initiative and was intended to justify not just the party's rule but his personal consolidation of power to a degree unprecedented since Mao Zedong and Deng Xiaoping.

A crucial aspect of the China Dream is the recovery of territory lost when China was weak and the restoration of the real or imagined status China enjoyed before the West intruded into Asia. The inconvenient fact, however, is that the most extensive territorial losses were to Imperial Russia and its successor states, which Xi now claims as his partner without limits. Siberia and what is now the Russian Far East are beyond even the pretence of recovery since the border was conclusively settled in 2003. What is left to impress the Chinese people with the CCP's resolve and success in defending China's sovereignty and territorial integrity are its claims to tiny islands, atolls, shoals, and reefs of the East and South China Seas, and Taiwan. The connection with the CCP's legitimacy gives its claims in the East and South China Seas far greater weight than the miniscule size of the land features or even potential undersea resources around them may suggest. Taiwan is of even greater political importance, and Xi has said several times that the China Dream cannot be achieved until Taiwan is reunified with China.

The deep sense of victimhood that permeates the CCP's legitimating narrative, and the presentation of the China Dream as the inevitable result of a historical process vouchsafed to the party, injects a strong element of entitlement into Chinese behaviour on these issues. It makes diplomatic compromise difficult except as a purely tactical and therefore temporary expedient.

Professor Yan Xuetong of Tsinghua University has spoken of the belief among the Chinese people that China's rise was 'granted by nature'.[55] One-time senior CCP member, diplomatic secretary to Premier Zhou Enlai, and Vice-President of the Chinese Academy of Social Sciences, Li Shenzhi, who turned critic after Tiananmen, once wrote: 'A *national mentality of self-importance* has been deeply rooted in people's minds as a result of over five decades of propaganda. Following the Reform and Open Door

Policy the economy has improved and with it has come a *blind arrogance and pride* . . . If we allow it to evolve freely, it may put the future of the nation at risk.' [emphasis added][56]

The CCP is caught in a trap of its own making. After all, having drummed into my people that I am only recovering what was stolen from me when I was weak, why should I compromise? And how can I defy the inevitable unfolding of History? What will my own people think of my mandate to rule if I bargain away what I claim was always mine?

These questions were less sensitive when China was growing rapidly. But China now faces a future of uninspiring growth. The three interrelated economic challenges confronting China – a precarious property sector that accounts for a quarter or more of GDP, burgeoning local government debt with consequent stresses on commercial banking, and a lack of confidence that has limited the effectiveness of the measures Beijing has taken to boost domestic consumption – are familiar and much discussed. But what is perhaps less well known or insufficiently stressed is that these issues are not only economic in form and are symptoms of a much more fundamental political challenge.

As early as 2007, then Premier Wen Jiabao warned that China's development was 'unstable, unbalanced, uncoordinated, and unsustainable'.[57] In 2012, in his last report to the CCP's 18th Congress – the same congress at which Xi Jinping took power – General Secretary Hu Jintao formally acknowledged that the economic model that had led to spectacular growth in the 1990s and first decade of the 2000s was unsustainable.[58]

That economic model relied on state-led investment in infrastructure to drive growth and created the glittering modern China that has drawn international admiration. These investments made sense in the 1990s and early 2000s when China had enormous need for new roads, airports, railways, offices, and housing. But a growth model that relies so heavily on infrastructure investment must eventually run out of productive investments and must wean itself lest debt rises faster than economic growth.

In 2013, the CCP rolled out a plan that envisaged a restructuring 'to allow the market to play a "decisive role" in the allocation of recourses'.[59] Very little of this 2013 plan has been implemented. Why? China has been talking about raising domestic consumption for more than a decade but the rate has stubbornly plateaued at under 40 per cent of GDP and it is not at all certain that the 'Special Action Plan' to stimulate domestic consumption announced in March 2025 will be any more successful than earlier measures. Again, one must ask: why?

The answer to both questions is not economic – China has scores of brilliant economists who have not only identified the problem but proposed solutions – it is political. There are no economic solutions to political problems.

China is a communist country. We sometimes forget this because it is so obvious as to hide in plain sight. Yet China is no longer ideologically communist. The CCP's legitimating ideology is now more strongly nationalist than orthodox Marxist or even Maoist. And while China's political structure clearly remains that of a Leninist state led by the CCP, the primary value of a Leninist-style vanguard party is political control, and the CCP insists on control over all aspects of state, economy, and society: the most core of China's core interests is to maintain CCP control. By definition, free markets mean less political control.

Political control and economic efficiency do not pose an absolute choice. What the 2013 plan required was a new balance between control and efficiency and it is this new balance that the CCP under Xi Jinping has been reluctant to establish. The first decade of Xi's rule has seen the CCP insist on ever more control over the economy, state, and society, tilting the balance in the opposite direction to that which the 2013 plan envisaged. Xi is clearly a true Leninist in that his almost Pavlovian response to problems seems to be 'more Party' and more control.[60] We saw this clearly in his stubborn insistence on continuing a Zero-Covid policy long beyond the point where it had become dysfunctional.

The expectations of the Chinese people have risen. At the 19th Party Congress in 2017, Xi himself acknowledged that the new 'principal challenge' facing China was the divide between 'unbalanced and inadequate development' and 'the requirements of the people to lead better lives', which had become 'increasingly broad'.[61] Xi set out a lengthy domestic agenda to meet those expectations. Dealing with that agenda in a country of China's size will require immense resources over a long time.

China may soon face a vicious circle if it is not already trapped in one. China must grow to acquire the resources to deal with rising expectations, but sustaining growth requires a new balance between political control and economic efficiency. Establishing that new balance requires the CCP to accept more political risk, mitigating those risks requires growth, and so on.

China is not about to collapse. The CCP is quite ingenious at adaptation. Xi has not given up on growth but continues to emphasise security and control. There was no sign at the 20th CCP Congress in 2022 or any subsequent high-level party meetings that Xi is contemplating anything more than tactical expedients to stimulate growth. Unless the party finds the political courage to break the vicious circle, the Chinese economy is going to operate sub-optimally. China will be pulled in contrary directions.

The competing imperatives were on full public display in February 2025. When confronted with a spluttering economy and lacklustre growth, Xi summoned Jack Ma of Alibaba, who had been at the centre of a crackdown on the tech industry a few years earlier, and told him and other private sector leaders that 'It is necessary to resolutely remove all kinds of obstacles to the equal use of production factors and fair participation in market competition.'[62] But less than two weeks later, Xi refocused attention on security when he told the Politburo that the top priority should be to 'safeguard the security of the regime, the political system, as well as ideology'.[63]

Little wonder then that China is facing a domestic and foreign crisis of confidence. Xi himself is the basic cause. The Chinese elite – intellectual, party, and business – are uncertain about the direction he is taking China, while rivalry with the United States adds geopolitical uncertainties into the equation for Chinese and foreign investors alike.

Xi's record of admitting mistakes during his first decade in power is not encouraging. He may make tactical adjustments to meet pressing immediate problems, as he did over Zero-Covid, which he abandoned only after demonstrations by students and workers (an ominous combination in modern Chinese history) broke out across the country. However, fundamental changes of policy under Xi seem unlikely. And regardless of whether or not he retains his formal titles at the next CCP Congress in 2027, Xi will probably call the shots for a long time, possibly until he is physically or mentally incapable of doing so. Concentrating power in his person also means concentrating responsibility. Xi's relentless anti-corruption campaign cannot but have created resentment and insecurity among elites, including in the PLA. Xi is riding a tiger of his own creation, and it is difficult to see how he can get off without being eaten.

By mid-century, whether or not Xi is still in power, long-term demographic factors will slow growth. The United Nations has projected that, on present trends, by the turn of the 21st century, China's population could be about halved. No big country in history has ever experienced such a precipitous fall in population and no country in the world has been able to reverse population decline due to falling birthrates. Technology is, at best, only a partial solution to a declining population. The only true solutions are immigration and the use of foreign labour. Neither is available to China on the scale needed.[64]

None of this means that we have reached 'peak China', whatever that phrase may mean. Even if China grows at around five per cent annually, that is roughly equivalent to adding another Australia to the world economy every year. Not a bad 'peak', if indeed it is one. Whether that will be sufficient to satisfy China's external ambitions and domestic expectations is a question only time can answer. And if insufficient, only time will tell how a frustrated China will behave.

What is certain is that the dilemmas facing China are real and have no easy solutions. Xi's emphasis on party discipline and control is not irrational. A huge country that has undergone profound transformation within only about 40 years is naturally internally roiled. An unstable China is in no one's interest. It is not clear that there is any practical alternative to CCP rule to maintain stability. But by emphasising CCP control, Xi has also sharpened the difficulty of finding a new balance for growth.

During the Hu Jintao period, the CCP recognised the limits of economic reform within a tight Leninist framework and cautiously experimented with more flexible political arrangements at the local level. The intention was to promote 'intra-party democracy' and bottom-up input in the selection and promotion of local party officials. Xi has foreclosed any significant modification of the political dynamics of a Leninist state.

A Leninist state is better placed to pursue a consistent long-term course. But since it is tilted towards control, change is almost always driven from the top. Bottom-up change is by definition threatening. Change is thus almost totally dependent on the quality and personality of the paramount leader and his decisions. In China, Mao's mistakes led to the disasters of the Great Leap Forward and the Cultural Revolution. Conversely, Deng Xiaoping was able to look dispassionately at his life's work, decide that it was going seriously wrong, and abruptly change course. Deng was able to change China with minimal political resistance because of the catastrophes Mao had brought upon the country. Change in Leninist systems may only come when they confront disaster.

Xi has abolished term limits and has time on his side. Unlike the Soviet Union, the Chinese system is adaptable and its economy more robust. But since 2012, Beijing's adaptations have been improvisations that circle around rather than directly address the core issue. This poses risks. The Chinese system could be reaching an inflection point where change cannot be indefinitely delayed without risking unpredictable and severe black swan-style events.

No leader has found the political will or courage to take the risks needed to break out of China's vicious circle by decisive action of the sort Deng took 40 years ago. Hu Jintao acknowledged the problem but ran out of time to implement the solution, and while Xi may be a genius at amassing power, his record of governance can at best be described as mixed, so he is unlikely to be such a leader.

The CCP is enormously powerful, with technological instruments of control of which Orwell could not even dream. But, paradoxically, it is also deeply and constantly insecure. China has, almost obsessively, studied the experience of the Soviet Union and its former East European satellites, the better to avoid their fate. Xi himself thought that the Soviet Union failed because at the end, no one among the Soviet leadership 'was man enough to stand up and resist'.[65] This goes a long way to explain his determination to concentrate power in his own person, his prioritisation of security, and his reluctance to confront the need to find a new stable equilibrium between control and efficiency.

But there is perhaps also a more profound reason for the insecurity that haunts the CCP. In his classic work, *From the Soil*, Chinese sociologist Fei Xiaotong explained the essential difference between Western and Chinese society by reference to China's rural foundations.[66] This led to the greater immediacy and importance of family and local networks centred on themselves rather than institutions of the state. As a result, Fei argued, Chinese society had a deeply ingrained 'self-centred quality' and traditional Chinese society was 'selfish'. Sun Yat-sen was suggesting much the same thing when he described the Chinese people as loose grains of sand. It is the root cause of the factionalism and localism that has always plagued the CCP.

Since 1949, the CCP has continually struggled to transform this deep social structure into something less personal and collective, turning to Marxism-Leninism, Maoism, Xi Jinping Thought for a New Era, and lately, even returning to Confucianism. The idea that economic growth was necessary to preserve CCP rule was Deng Xiaoping's insight, and it probably saved the CCP. But what Deng could not foresee was that as reform progressed, it also increased the space and scope for individual agency and personal networks, and thus for old modes of behaviour – or, to use Fei's term, 'selfishness' – to reassert themselves and compete with the CCP's authority and the kind of unified, collective identity it wanted to promote.

Can a Leninist state tolerate this? China has, up to a point. The lives of the Chinese people grew steadily freer and more prosperous after reforms began. This undoubtedly made the CCP popular. But broader scope for 'selfish' individual agency also created ample opportunity for corruption. Any rule and every control became an opportunity for circumvention; the vanguard party's immense power was a temptation to its members to monetise their authority. By the end of Hu Jintao's term, corruption reached into the highest levels of the system. This led to growing public disillusionment that threatened to undermine the CCP's legitimacy.

Xi's initial mandate was to bring corruption under control. One of his first initiatives was to stress the role of law in governance. But in a Leninist system, where the party is the supreme authority, governance can only be rule *by* law and never *of* law because the latter gives the law an autonomous authority above the party. Xi Jinping quickly began to use the anti-corruption campaign to accumulate power and has used the CCP's disciplinary apparatus to force cadres to comply with his will.

Xi's will is now closely identified with the party's will, much as it was during Mao's last phase. Xi is nevertheless *not* Mao redux. Mao was a revolutionary romantic, even prepared to destroy the party if it was an obstacle to his volitions. Xi is an apparatchik who sees strengthening the CCP as the key to overcoming China's challenges and fulfilling China's ambitions. But Xi's concentration of power may have reintroduced into the Chinese system something akin to a neo-Maoist single point of failure, in which a bad decision by an individual or a small group can have a disproportionate system-wide effect.

China will have to grapple with these internal contradictions within the context of global geopolitics that have returned to the historical norm of rivalry between major powers. Throughout China's history, the moments of maximum danger for dynasties are when periods of internal uncertainty coincide with external uncertainties. Are we in such a moment? Nothing is clear, except perhaps that as formidable as China undoubtedly is, its future can no longer be regarded as an Asian version of the Whig interpretation of history: a story of continual progress.

CHAPTER FIVE

So, whose century is it?

Thus far, this Paper has focused on the United States and China with only passing references to other Asian countries. US-China relations are the single most significant factor in 21st-century geopolitics, but it is not the whole of geopolitics, and certainly not in such a diverse continent as Asia. This concluding chapter will add a final layer of complexity to the idea of the Asian 21st century by bringing other Asian countries into our analysis. But the role of any country must be seen in wider perspective. As ought to be evident by now, I do not think that Asia or any part of it can be usefully considered in isolation from broader historical and geopolitical trends.

American-led globalisation gave rise to the prospect of a new American 'empire'. That soon proved illusory, although some of the early moves by

Trump 2.0 (for example, talk of annexing Greenland and retaking control of the Panama Canal) can be seen as an attempt to revive that idea. China's rise and Xi's ambitious Belt and Road Initiative (BRI) have generated analogous expectations of a new Chinese empire and the reestablishment, on a grander scale, of its tributary system.[67] 'Empire' and 'tributary system' are of course only metaphors and not to be taken literally. But they assume that the outcome of US-China competition will be some form of consolidation of international order, just as the world coalesced around the United States and the Soviet Union into the bipolar order of the Cold War.

This is unlikely.

The Cold War structure was clearly bipolar. The universal ideologies professed by the United States and the Soviet Union were intended to consolidate the centrality of their respective Romes. But the dynamics of Cold War competition were very quickly shaped by nationalism into more complex patterns. Within the boundaries of a state, nationalism is unifying; externally, it is a centrifugal force. It was to prove more compelling than either universal ideology, and both the United States and the Soviet Union struggled against it.

Since the end of the First World War, and more insistently as the 20th century unfolded, fragmentation rather than consolidation has been the most salient characteristic of the international system. There were three main waves of fragmentation: after the First World War when self-determination was established as a principle of international relations and old empires broke up; after the Second World War as the remaining empires were swept away by decolonisation; and after the Soviet Union fragmented. Putin is swimming against the current of world history if he is trying to reestablish the Soviet empire. So is China if Xi is dreaming of restoring China's place in an old Asian hierarchy.

The number of states expanded with each wave. At its height, the League of Nations had 63 members. The United Nations started in 1945 with 51 members. By 1980, when post-war decolonisation was almost complete, the United Nations had 154 members. In 1992, a year after the USSR ended, membership had grown to 179. Today, the United Nations has 193 members and two observers. To expect that an international system of such great diversity will neatly settle into a binary or any simple pattern in Asia or anywhere else is a fantasy.

The Soviet bloc developed cracks as early as 1948, when Yugoslavia charted its own course. In 1953, 1956, and 1968, Moscow had to intervene to crush revolts in East Germany, Hungary, and

Czechoslovakia respectively. The Sino-Soviet split was the prime example of how nationalism overrode ideology. Conflict erupted along their border and the possibility of all-out war was real. Moscow reportedly sounded out the United States on its response if Russia was to launch an attack on Chinese nuclear facilities.[68] Beijing, unwilling to subordinate itself to Moscow, was prepared to make common cause with the main capitalist devil against its fraternal socialist brother.

The more elastic American system generally did not need drastic action to hold together. But France was always unruly, and Europe as a whole needed persistent cajoling to speak with one voice. The United States constantly struggled, by covert and overt means, to herd its cats in the Third World. Vietnam exemplified America's inability to subdue nationalism, and it had to ignominiously withdraw. Thirteen years later, the Soviet Union suffered the same fate in Afghanistan. For Moscow, the consequences of defeat were systemic. It was the beginning of the end of the Soviet Union.

Moscow ruled with the knout. The United States was not averse to using force but generally used less direct methods, with economics its preferred tool. In the immediate post-war period, the Marshall Plan was crucial in tying both shores of the Atlantic together. The United States opened its markets to friends and allies in Asia and elsewhere to strengthen their economies and undermine the appeal of communism.

American generosity began to wear thin by the 1980s, but by that time the economic superiority of markets to deliver prosperity had led many countries around the world to develop variants (not carbon copies) of the American economic model and more or less voluntarily attach themselves to the United States. This was a strategic advantage, but one that ordinary Americans did not always see as being of benefit to their daily concerns. The hub-and-spokes system of formal military alliances stiffened this structure, but was never the whole of it. Post-Mao China was part of this system, and its chief beneficiary. As the Cold War waned, this led to a nationalist backlash in the United States that Trump shrewdly harnessed to gain power. Now that post-Cold War America is not prepared to bear the burdens of underpinning this system, can China take its place, as Xi has occasionally hinted?

To pose the question is tantamount to asking whether a global system that is essentially open can be led by a still largely closed economy. The root cause of that largely closed system is the privileged position of the CCP. Can that position be altered without risking the entire Chinese system? That is the core issue confronting the CCP's global ambitions. Until the CCP decides what risks it is prepared to take, Chinese global leadership will be partial, patchy, and never uncontested.

The experience of the Cold War years suggests that nationalism and the progressive fragmentation of the international system will pose complicated challenges to any major power with aspirations of global leadership. There is no a priori reason why China should be exempt. Unless major powers act sensitively, their nationalism will engender resentment and resistance from other nationalisms. The United States and China both consider themselves exceptional, but neither country's nationalism is renowned for sensitivity to other cultures. Insensitivity is perhaps the primary characteristic of the current leaders of both countries.

Some nationalisms will be more problematic than others. There are two main types of nationalism: civic and ethnic. Civic nationalism is based on attachment to universal principles that are in theory open to all to accept; ethnic nationalism is based on blood and, to a lesser extent, on culture, with culture primarily defined by ethnicity.

In theory, the United States and Soviet Union were both based on civic nationalism. In practice, ethnic

Russian nationalism quickly became dominant in the Soviet Union. This was one reason why Soviet control of its bloc necessitated more direct use of force or threat of force, particularly in Eastern Europe and with China, where Russian nationalism confronted another nationalism that traditionally and over centuries considered itself superior to every other, even when it lacked power.

China's nationalism is in principle civic nationalism of the Soviet communist type. In practice, the revanchist historical narratives of victimhood, rejuvenation, and final redemption through achieving the China Dream, which the CCP aggressively promotes to legitimate its rule, turn civic nationalism into Han ethnic nationalism.

The CCP appeals to civic nationalism in a pro-forma way when dealing with China's own ethnic minorities. But even then, Chinese nationalism in practice means Sinicisation, particularly with Uighurs and Tibetans, whose numbers are too large to tolerate as a separate identity. Xi has tried to Sinicise these minorities with greater insistence and brutality than any of his predecessors since Mao.

What is China? Who is Chinese? In the late 19th century, under pressure to accept Western concepts of international relations, the Qing Emperor drew a line around what was then the extent of his domain and called it 'China'. It would take a while before the supple frontiers – mental as well as physical – of an empire could be transformed into the clearly delineated fixed boundaries of a state. It waxed and waned over time, and in theory encompassed all under heaven. In practice, that process is not yet complete.[69]

Who is Chinese? What is China? These remain questions without straightforward answers. As China seeks a bigger global role, the CCP's attempts to force these complex questions into rigid categories determined by an ideological interpretation of its history creates liabilities, as it is not very appealing to non-Chinese. China's Global Security Initiative, Global Development Initiative, and Global Civilisational Initiative are unconvincing attempts to at least mitigate these liabilities by the use of more universal concepts. But the CCP's use of a legitimating narrative infused with a sense of entitlement and cultural superiority, and the implicit expectation of subordination that is its consequence, still often makes Chinese foreign policy clumsy and tone-deaf. Yet China has no credible alternative to this narrative.

During the Cold War, American civic nationalism was sometimes very intrusive. Well-meaning but naïve and impatient Americans annoyingly tried to nag or nudge their friends in what they believed was the 'correct' direction of political development; this occasionally erupted into coercion when the instinct to whip the heathen along the path of righteousness became too strong to be resisted. But on the whole, American civic nationalism was easier for other countries to live with as long as America pretended to minimally observe the principles it professed.

More recently, however, American civic nationalism is being contested by an aggressive ethnic nationalism that asserts a white, Christian identity as more authentically American. Trump symbolises, encourages, and exploits this trend. The early stages of this shift were described by the historian Arthur M. Schlesinger Jr in his book *The Disuniting of America*, first published in 1991 as the Cold War ended.[70]

Where this shift will lead America is not clear. It does not seem very likely that the more extreme variants of American ethic nationalism will prevail, even though ideas once considered unrespectable are no longer beyond the pale. America is already too ethnically diverse a society to be reduced to the monochromatic America some nationalists see as the ideal, and there are inherent informal checks and balances in America's messiness. But even if it remains primarily civic, post-Cold War American nationalism has already become narrower and more transactional, and this will persist.

Globalisation facilitates fragmentation: first because its disruptions and the immediacy with which the alien 'other' intrudes into life arouse strong emotions of separateness; and second, it enables inchoate emotions to crystalise into statehood because in principle, if not always in practice, it makes small polities that are able to plug into global networks viable. Singapore is one of the earliest and most successful examples.

In the 21st century, we may be entering into a fourth wave of fragmentation as identity politics of various kinds breeds new types of communal emotions, some of which may eventually coagulate into national or quasi-national forms, while others will ebb and flow across national boundaries, changing form as they do. A world of proliferating and fluid identities will be a more complex world for both China and the United States to deal with, although perhaps somewhat more challenging for China's ethnic nationalism than the so far still primarily civic American nationalism.

As they try to navigate these broad trends and the complexities that swathe the seemingly straightforward idea of an Asian century, every country in

Asia is confronted with two fundamental strategic realities.

First, the United States and China are geopolitical facts that cannot be ignored. There is an increasing appreciation that dealing with both simultaneously is a necessary condition of dealing with either effectively. Without a relationship with the United States, we will deal with China in such a state of disequilibrium that our autonomy will be in serious jeopardy. But without a relationship with China, a more transactional United States will take our interests for granted. Our relations with the United States and China will need to be delicately calibrated to keep them in some form of balance that does not tip too far one way or another. This will be difficult, but there is no alternative.

Second, there are concerns about *both* American and Chinese behaviour. The concerns are not the same nor are they held with the same intensity. The nature of the concerns and their intensity will vary across countries and will change over time as circumstances and the policies of the United States and China evolve. But concerns about both will never be absent in Asia.

Faced with these dual realities, most countries in Asia are going to try to maximise strategic flexibility within the constraints of their circumstances.

No country anywhere, even formal US allies or those economically dependent on China, will want to align all their interests across all domains in one direction or another. They will try to align different interests in different domains in the most advantageous direction. Since all countries face the same imperative, no country's choices need be confined to only the United States or China. The United States and China may be the most important actors but they are not the only potential partners.

As the 21st century progresses, a system of what could be termed asymmetrical dynamic multipolarity (ADM) could evolve. The US-China relationship will be the main axis around which eclectic clusters of countries will continually form, dissolve, and reconstitute themselves as their interests dictate. States must learn to understand equilibrium dynamically – as continual motion to adjust to other motions that will in turn adjust to our adjustments – not as a static balance.

These domain-defined coalitions or clusters will not all be of the same weight and should not be measured by traditional indices of population, GDP, or military might but by their competencies in specific domains. Middle-sized or even small countries could carry weight in specific domains or on particular issues. Some may include both the United States and China, some will include one or the other, and some neither. Japan, India, Australia, South Korea, Indonesia, Vietnam, and even some of the smaller ASEAN members could potentially play crucial roles in this emerging ADM structure.[71]

Several developments already tentatively point in this direction. Japan and Australia took the initiative to form the Comprehensive and Progressive Agreement for Trans-Pacific Partnership (CPTPP) after the first Trump administration renounced the Trans-Pacific Partnership. India joined the Quad out of concern about China, but those concerns did not prevent India from also joining the China-led Shanghai Cooperation Organisation because of its interests in Central Asia. India left the ASEAN-led Regional Comprehensive Economic Partnership (RCEP), but along with the United States, China, and Russia, among others, is part of other ASEAN-initiated forums such as the East Asia Summit and the ASEAN Defence Ministers' Meeting Plus.

Since Asia is the epicentre of the broad shifts occurring in global politics – the rise of China and India; the deep and pervasive influence of US-China competition; the global web of supply chains – it will be the test-bed for this emerging ADM system, which could eventually spread to other regions. This may therefore become the most accurate version of the term 'Asian century'.

Such a fluid and multi-faceted system cannot be geographically constrained. The trends driving the evolution of ADM are global. Implicit in all I have said is that geography is becoming less relevant as an indicator of political or strategic alignment. Membership of many of the forums and institutions I have mentioned is already not confined to Asia. Japan, South Korea, and Australia are taking a greater interest in NATO and have attended its summits. The European Union, France, Germany, and the Netherlands have issued Indo-Pacific strategy papers. The United Kingdom has joined the CPTPP and the European Union too has expressed interest in it. This cannot be a purely Asian 'Asian century'.

ADM will not displace existing alliances, institutions, and forums, but form an overlay that shapes their dynamics and in turn will be shaped by them. But ADM will also emerge on a foundation of a new multipolar form of nuclear deterrence.

North Korea's development of nuclear weapon and missile capabilities and, more importantly, China's modernisation of its nuclear forces, are bound in time to erode the credibility of American extended deterrence over its Asian allies. Asian versions of the question Charles de Gaulle posed in Europe decades ago – will San Francisco or Los Angeles be sacrificed to save Tokyo or Seoul? – are beginning to be asked in Asia, whispered behind locked doors in Japan, but openly discussed in Seoul where opinion polls show strong support for South Korea acquiring an independent nuclear deterrent.[72]

Both countries could acquire such a capability in a relatively short time once a decision is made.[73] There is some reason to believe that Tokyo has been quietly preparing for such a contingency for decades, with American acquiescence if not active encouragement. The US-Japan nuclear cooperation agreement of 1987 is unique among all such US agreements in permitting Japan to reprocess uranium. There is only one reason why any country should want to do so. In any case, Japan already has a stockpile of almost 50 tons of plutonium, a fissile material, acquiring which is the most difficult step for any country with nuclear weapons ambitions.[74]

Neither Japan nor South Korea is eager to build nuclear weapons, but the logic of their strategic circumstances will inexorably drive them in that direction. In my judgement, it is not a matter of whether but when Japan and South Korea become nuclear powers. It will almost certainly happen well within the remaining years of the 21st century. Acquiring independent nuclear deterrents is the only way for Tokyo and Seoul to avoid subordination to Beijing and the eventual break-up of the US alliance system in Asia. During the 2016 US election campaign, Trump floated the idea of Japan and South Korea acquiring nuclear weapons as a cheaper way to defend them. An America that defines its interests narrowly and transactionally will catalyse such decisions.

In Europe, the shock of Trump's determination to force a stop to the fighting in Ukraine has caused Polish leaders to muse aloud about getting access to nuclear weapons.[75] Among the casualties of the Ukraine war is the non-proliferation regime because it is clear that if Kyiv had not been so naïve as to give up the nuclear weapons it inherited from the Soviet Union in return for worthless paper security guarantees, it would not be in the existential bind it is in today.

After the Russian invasion of 2022, the late Abe Shinzo, speaking in the Diet, suggested that Japan allow American tactical nuclear weapons to be stationed on its territory.[76] In a different time, there would have been an uproar. But his suggestion evoked relatively little controversy, a remarkable change in public attitudes. It will be politically difficult for Japan, the only country to have suffered a nuclear attack and where there is still a strong current of pacifism, to develop its own nuclear weapons. But since the 19th century, Japan has demonstrated an ability to shift strategic direction abruptly when national survival is at stake.

Asia's diversity and its instinct to simultaneously hedge, balance, and bandwagon makes it a naturally multipolar region. The road to the emergence of a nuclear balance between the United States, China, Russia, North Korea, Japan, South Korea, India, Pakistan, and possibly Australia will be fraught with tensions that will have to be managed. But the end result will be stabilising, as the historical record of nuclear balances has shown. No nuclear-weapon state has gone to war with another nuclear-weapon state. A nuclear balance will freeze the region's multipolar configuration, making it impossible for China or any other power to impose a hierarchical structure on it. There will not be an Asian century but a century of multiple Asias.

CHAPTER SIX

Conclusions

The theme running through this Paper is that the story of Asia since the early 20th century is the recovery and enhancement of agency. This is what Jan Romein meant when he titled his book *The Asian Century*. But the rise of nationalism is not particularly 'Asian'. Some Asian states were among the first to shake off their colonial masters in the 20th century, but Latin America was even earlier, gaining independence from Spain in the 19th century. By the end of the 20th century, Africa and the Middle East were free, too.

The idea of the recovery of agency nevertheless moves us closer to the crux of what the idea of an 'Asian century' signifies. Asian countries now have to be dealt with in their own right and not as accessories to some other concern. Asia matters not only insofar as it affects Europe, as during the colonial era; not as an arena of US-Soviet competition during the Cold War; and not as a blank sheet where contests between ideas claimed as universal play out regardless of specific contexts of history and culture.

China, India, Japan, Korea, Vietnam, and Indonesia, to name but a few, are countries with long histories and deep pride in their cultures. They are never going to be anybody's tool or play deputy to any sheriff, and are not mere representations of abstractions. To state the obvious – which nevertheless is still often ignored – they have their own interests and the agency to advance them.

The mental transition from thinking of 'Asia' only as an arena to thinking about Asian countries as actors is still incomplete, as the continuing appeal of the 'Asian century' trope itself demonstrates. Simplistic binaries such as contrasting the 'Asian century' with the 'American century', or the starker Chinese version of 'the East rising and the West declining', objectify the countries involved, brush aside their diversity, and reduce them to mere representations of whatever larger forces may strike one's fancy.

The countries of Asia have not always used their agency well or wisely. That is to be expected since they are real places populated by real people who hope and fear, succeed and fail, soar to the greatest heights and plummet to the darkest depths of which humans are capable. In doing so, they act and react to each other and thus change their hopes and fears, their successes and failures, their ambitions and their insecurities, in an ever-shifting kaleidoscope of contingencies and possibilities.

The alert reader will have noticed that apart from the introduction and this conclusion, all of my chapter titles are questions. There are no definitive answers to most of the questions I have raised, although I have ventured some speculations. If the reader, having intrepidly ploughed through to the end of this essay, now finds himself or herself lost in doubt about whether there is, or can ever be, an Asian century, this essay has achieved its purpose.

Some will no doubt find this unsatisfactory. But before you ask for your money back, I must remind you of a thought experiment conducted in 1935 by the Austrian physicist Erwin Schrödinger, in which a cat is locked in a box with a capsule of cyanide that has a 50 per cent chance of breaking and killing the cat. Until the box is opened and we can see what has happened, the cat is in an indeterminate state of being both alive and dead. The Asian box is still closed and so not only is the Asian cat neither alive nor dead, it may not even be a cat.

Acknowledgements

As always, I write primarily for my children. My daughter, Catherine Kamala Wei Sin P.S. Kausikan, already knows all that appears in these pages, and more. To my son, David Raman Wei Siong P.S. Kausikan, these were some of the things I wanted to tell you but didn't have the chance.

Endnotes

1 The phrase was coined by Ezra Vogel, *The Four Little Dragons: The Spread of Industrialization in East Asia*, (Harvard University Press, 1991).

2 Acceptance is not total – in Japan and South Korea, 'East Asia' still often means only themselves and China. The distinction between the 'dragons' of South Korea, Taiwan, Hong Kong, and Singapore, and the 'tigers' of Indonesia, Malaysia, and Thailand, makes a similar point. In reality, tigers range as far north as Siberia, and dragons are not unknown in the mythologies of Southeast Asia, where they are called naga.

3 For example, see Staffan Burenstam Linder, *The Pacific Century: Economic and Political Consequences of Asian-Pacific Dynamism*, (Stanford University Press, 1986).

4 See, for example, 'An expose of how states manipulate other countries' citizens' and 'How China messes with your mind' in Bilahari Kausikan, *Singapore is Still Not an Island: More Views on Singapore Foreign Policy*,

(Straits Times Press, 2023), pp. 150–6 and 134–49. Also, Joshua Kurlantzick, *Beijing's Global Media Offensive: China's Uneven Campaign to Influence Asia and the World*, (Oxford University Press, 2022).

5 Donald Low, '"Born-Again" Chinese: Singapore's PRC Apologists', *Academia SG*, 8 March 2025, academia.sg/academic-views/born-again-chinese-of-singapore. The phenomenon Mr Low described is not confined to Singapore.

6 'Evolving a Foreign Policy for Singapore', unpublished lecture by Senior Minister in the Prime Minister's Office Mr S. Rajaratnam at the Institute of Policy Studies, Singapore, 12 July 1988.

7 *Selected Works of Deng Xiaoping*, Volume III, (Foreign Languages Press, 1994) pp. 274–6.

8 Jan Romein, *The Asian Century: A History of Modern Nationalism in Asia*, English translation, (University of California Press, 1962).

9 Henry Luce, 'The American Century', *Life*, 17 February 1941, pp. 61–5.

10 The other pillars of the American post-war order were provided by NATO and US alliances in Asia. However, the UN and Bretton Woods systems were unique in that they were intended, at least in principle, to serve not just American interests but the common interests of all countries.

11 Francis Fukuyama, 'The End of History?', *The National Interest*, Number 16, Summer 1989, pp. 3–18. When 'History' stubbornly refused to conform to the good professor's theories, he wrote a whole book to prove

that history, in his special use of the term, had indeed ended but the rest of us were insufficiently erudite to understand or even notice. Francis Fukuyama, *The End of History and the Last Man*, (The Free Press, 1992).

12 For an elaboration, see Bilahari Kausikan, 'Asia's Different Standard', *Foreign Policy*, Number 92, Fall 1993, pp. 24–41; and Bilahari Kausikan, 'The Myth of Universality: The Geopolitics of Human Rights', in Bilahari Kausikan, *Dealing with an Ambiguous World*, (World Scientific, 2016), pp. 93–122.

13 Xi Jinping, 'Towards an Asian Century of Prosperity', *The Hindu*, 17 September 2014 (updated 20 April 2016), thehindu.com/opinion/op-ed/towards-an-asian-century-of-prosperity/article6416553.ece.

14 For a useful overview of Sino-Indian tensions, see Vappala Balachandran, *India and China at Odds in the Asian Century: A Diplomatic and Strategic History*, (Hurst, 2025).

15 See Victor G. Kiernan, *The Lords of Human Kind: European Attitudes to the Outside World in the Imperial Age*, (Penguin, 1972).

16 Kakuzo Okakura, *The Ideals of the East, with Special Reference to the Art of Japan*, (John Murray, 1903), p. 1.

17 For example, see Stephen N. Hay, *Asian Ideas of East and West: Tagore and his Critics in Japan, China, and India*, (Harvard University Press, 1970).

18 Gopa Sabharwal, 'In Search of an Asian Vision: The Asian Relations Conference of 1947', in Andrea Acri

et al (eds), *Imagining Asia(s)*, (ISEAS – Yusof Ishak Institute, 2019), pp. 60–90.

19 Nancy M. Birdsall et al, *The East Asian Miracle: Economic Growth and Public Policy*, (New York: Oxford University Press for the World Bank, 1993), documents.worldbank.org/curated/en/975081468244550798.

20 Richard Stubbs, *Rethinking Asia's Economic Miracle: The Political Economy of War, Prosperity and Crisis*, (Palgrave, 2005).

21 For details, see Chung Min Lee, *Fault Lines in a Rising Asia*, (Carnegie Endowment for International Peace, 2016); Vasuki Shastry, *Has Asia Lost It? Dynamic Past, Turbulent Future*, (World Scientific, 2021); and Jong-Wha Lee, *Is This the Asian Century?*, (World Scientific, 2017).

22 As cited in John West, *Asian Century on a Knife's Edge*, (Palgrave, 2018), pp. 2–3. West cited Kishore Mahbubani as an example of what he called Asian century 'hype'.

23 Zhao Ziwen and Dewey Sim, 'China's "Two Sessions" 2023: Chinese Development "Shatters" Modern-is-Western Myth, Foreign Minister Qin Gang Says', *South China Morning Post*, 7 March 2023, scmp.com/news/china/diplomacy/article/3212712/chinas-two-sessions-chinese-development-shatters-modern-western-myth-foreign-minister-qin-gang-says.

24 'Secure a Decisive Victory in Building a Moderately Prosperous Society in All Respects and Strive for the Great Success of Socialism with Chinese Characteristics for a New Era', speech delivered by Xi Jinping at the

19th National Congress of the Communist Party of China, in Xi Jinping, *The Governance of China, Vol III*, (Foreign Languages Press, 2020) p. 12.

25 'Khrushchev Tirade Again Irks Envoys', *New York Times*, 19 November 1956, p. 1, nytimes.com/1956/11/19/archives/khrushchev-tirade-again-irks-envoys-khrushcaev-gibe-irks-envoys.html.

26 John Maynard Keynes, *The Economic Consequences of the Peace*, (independently republished, 2020), p. 6.

27 Chinese company Huawei has made advances in producing high-end chips to replace those manufactured by US firm NVIDIA, but the failure rate is reportedly high. See 'Huawei Faces Production Challenges with 20% Yield Rate for AI Chip', *TrendForce*, 28 June 2024, trendforce.com/news/2024/06/28/news-huawei-faces-production-challenges-with-20-yield-rate-for-ai-chip/. Critically, in the production of high-end chips, there does not seem to be any viable alternative to ASML photolithography machines, which are Dutch.

28 Kate O'Keeffe, 'US Approves Nearly All Tech Exports to China, Data Shows', *Wall Street Journal*, 16 August 2022, wsj.com/politics/national-security/u-s-approves-nearly-all-tech-exports-to-china-data-shows-11660596886.

29 President John F. Kennedy's Inaugural Address, 1961, archives.gov/milestone-documents/president-john-f-kennedys-inaugural-address.

30 See Douglas A. Irwin, *Clashing over Commerce: A History of US Trade Policy*, (University of Chicago Press, 2019).

31 Fenella McGerty, 'Asian Defence Spending Grows, China Grows More', International Institute for Strategic Studies, 22 May 2024, search.app/q7Qu2zUptc8eyfYN8.

32 'Foreign Relations of the United States, 1969–1976, Volume X, Vietnam, January 1973–July 1975, Minutes of Cabinet Meeting', US Department of State, Washington, 16 April 1975, search.app/HjUBau9ja10FZ233A.

33 See 'Moral Man and Immoral Society' and 'The Irony of American History' in Reinhold Niebuhr, *Major Works on Religion and Politics*, (Library of America, 2015).

34 See Tripp Mickle, 'TSMC, the Chip Giant, is to Spend $100 Billion in US over the Next 4 Years', *The New York Times*, 3 March 2025, nytimes.com/2025/03/03/technology/tsmc-investment-trump.html; and Jack Ewing, 'Hyundai to Invest $21 Billion in US in Bid to Avoid Trump's Tariffs', *The New York Times*, 24 March 2025, nytimes.com/2025/03/24/business/hyundai-us-investment-tariffs.html.

35 Chun Han Wong, 'Putin, Xi Reaffirm Ties on Anniversary of Ukraine War', *The Wall Street Journal*, 24 February 2025, wsj.com/world/russia/putin-xi-reaffirm-ties-on-ukraine-war-anniversary-74d758e7.

36 Bilahari Kausikan, 'The Indo-Pacific after Donald Trump', *Nikkei Asia*, 17 January 2021, asia.nikkei.com/Opinion/The-Indo-Pacific-after-Donald-Trump.

37 Lingling Wei, Rebecca Feng, and Raffaele Huang, 'China's Xi is Angered by Panama Port Deal that Trump Touted as a Win', *Wall Street Journal*, 18 March 2025, wsj.com/world/china/

chinas-xi-is-angered-by-panama-port-deal-that-trump-touted-as-a-win-9a0c22fe.

38 US Department of Defense, Remarks by Secretary of Defense Pete Hegseth at the 2025 Shangri-La Dialogue in Singapore (As Delivered), 31 May 2025, defense.gov/News/Speeches/Speech/Article/4202494/remarks-by-secretary-of-defense-pete-hegseth-at-the-2025-shangri-la-dialogue-in/.

39 Bilahari Kausikan, 'Trump's Next Deal Should be with Kim Jong Un', *Foreign Policy*, 26 February 2025, foreignpolicy.com/2025/02/26/trump-kim-north-korea-nuclear-diplomacy-deal.

40 Michael J. Green, *By More Than Providence: Grand Strategy and American Power in the Asia-Pacific Since 1783*, (Columbia University Press, 2017), p. 5.

41 Aileen S. P. Baviera, 'Power Asymmetry in South China Sea', *Inquirer.Net*, 2011, /opinion.inquirer.net/6896/power-asymmetry-in-south-china-sea/amp; and Ian Storey, 'China's Missteps in Southeast Asia: Less Charm, More Offensive', in *China Brief*, Volume 10, Issue 25, 17 December 2010.

42 Zhang Zheng Bijian, 'China's "Peaceful Rise" to Great-Power Status', *Foreign Affairs*, September/October 2005, foreignaffairs.com/articles/asia/2005-09-01/chinas-peaceful-rise-great-power-status.

43 Wang Huning, *Meiguo Fandui Meiguo*, (1992). As far as I know, there is no official translation, but I have access to a PDF of an unofficial translation.

44 Philippine President Ferdinand Marcos Jr has given US forces access to several new facilities, allowed the

deployment of American intermediate-range missile launchers on Philippines territory, and acquired anti-ship missiles from India. Indonesia has sent troops to participate in the US-Australia Talisman Saber exercises, scaled up its own Super Garuda Shield series of exercises with the United States, in which Japan and Australia also participate, and in 2023 announced that it would acquire F-15 fighters and Black Hawk helicopters from the United States. Vietnam has allowed port calls from US aircraft carriers and is reportedly in talks to buy US weapons systems. When it is too sensitive to work directly with the United States, Southeast Asian countries have expanded ties with US allies, principally Japan and Australia. Of all the ASEAN members, only Laos has unequivocally thrown in its lot with China. Cambodia is still hedging between the United States and China.

45 Lynn Kuok, 'America is Losing Southeast Asia: Why US Allies in the Region are Turning toward China', *Foreign Affairs*, 3 September 2024, foreignaffairs.com/united-states/america-losing-southeast-asia.

46 Sharon Seah et al, *The State of Southeast Asia: 2024 Survey Report*, (ISEAS – Yusof Ishak Institute, 2024), p. 48. The results of the 2025 survey are consistent with this general pattern, which has held since the survey began in 2019.

47 Sharon Seah et al, *The State of Southeast Asia: 2025 Survey Report*, (ISEAS – Yusof Ishak Institute, 2025), p. 46.

48 In the 2024 survey, 43.9 per cent of respondents rated China the most influential political and strategic power, and almost 60 per cent rated China the most influential

economic power in Southeast Asia. The comparable figures for the United States were only 25.8 per cent and 14.3 per cent. But 67.4 per cent of those surveyed were uneasy about China's economic influence, and even more – 73.5 per cent – were worried about China's political and strategic influence. More than half of ASEAN (50.1 per cent) had little or no confidence that China would 'do the right thing' to contribute to global peace, security, prosperity, and governance, while only 24.8 per cent were confident or very confident that China would do so. The comparable figures for the United States were 37.6 per cent and 42.4 per cent. As far as overall trust in external powers is concerned, in 2024, 42.4 per cent chose the United States as compared to only 24.8 per cent opting for China. Ibid, particularly pp. 56–67.

49 Ibid, pp. 44, 54.

50 Two honourable exceptions whose works are indispensable to anyone seeking to understand the complexity of Southeast Asian attitudes towards China and other major powers are Murray Hiebert, *Under Beijing's Shadow: Southeast Asia's China Challenge*, (Center for Strategic and International Studies, 2020) and Thomas Parks, *Southeast Asia's Multipolar Future: Averting a New Cold War*, (Bloomsbury Academic, 2023).

51 The changes in the strategic environment are primarily China's rise and a more transactional post-Cold War America. See Bilahari Kausikan, 'Abe's Legacy: An Appreciation', in *Singapore is Still Not an Island: More Views on Singapore Foreign Policy*, (Straits Times Press, 2023), pp. 233–41.

52 See S. Jaishankar, *The India Way: Strategies for an Uncertain World*, (HarperCollins India, 2020) and Shivshankar Menon, *India in a World Adrift*, Lowy Institute Paper, (Penguin, 2025).

53 See 'Telling China's Story Well', *China Media Project*, 16 April 2021, china media project.org/the_ccp_dictionary/telling-chinas-story-well/; and 'Xi Jinping Calls for More "Lovable" Image for China in Bid to Make Friends', BBC News, 2 June 2021, bbc.com/news/world-asia-china-57327177.amp.

54 For example, Wang Jisi, 'Has the US Really Declined? Chinese Need to Have a Clear Understanding about This', 14 May 2022, gaodawei.wordpress.com/2022/06/01/wang-jisi-has-the-u-s-really-declined-chinese-need-to-have-a-clear-understanding-about-this/.

55 Yan Xuetong, 'The Rise of China in Chinese Eyes', *Journal of Contemporary China*, Volume 10, Issue 26, 2001, pp. 33–9.

56 Li Shenzhi, 'On the Diplomacy of the People's Republic of China', as cited in John W. Garver, *China's Quest: The History of the Foreign Relations of the People's Republic of China*, (Oxford University Press, 2016), p. 783.

57 Tom Holland, 'Wen and Now: China's Economy is Still "Unsustainable"', *South China Morning Post*, 10 April 2017, scmp.com/week-asia/opinion/article/2085815/wen-and-now-chinas-economy-still-unsustainable.

58 Hu Jintao, 'Report to the 18th National Congress of the Communist Party of China: Firmly March on the Path of Socialism with Chinese Characteristics and Strive to Complete the Building of a Moderately Prosperous

Society in all Respects', 8 November 2012, chinadaily.com.cn/china/19thcpcnationalcongress/2012-11/18/content_29578562.htm.

59 Cary Huang, 'Party's Third Plenum Pledges "Decisive Role" for Markets in China's Economy', *South China Morning Post*, 12 November 2013, scmp.com/news/china/article/1354411/chinas-leadership-approves-key-reform-package-close-third-plenum.

60 On Xi Jinping's Leninist beliefs, see Kevin Rudd, *On Xi Jinping: How Xi's Marxist Nationalism is Shaping China and the World*, (Oxford University Press, 2024).

61 'Secure a Decisive Victory in Building a Moderately Prosperous Society in All Respects and Strive for the Great Success of Socialism with Chinese Characteristics for a New Era', speech delivered by Xi Jinping at the 19th National Congress of the Communist Party of China, in Xi Jinping, *The Governance of China, Vol III*, (Foreign Languages Press, 2020) pp. 12–13.

62 'Xi Voices Support for Jack Ma, China Private Sector Chiefs', Bloomberg News, 17 February 2025, bloomberg.com/news/articles/2025-02-17/xi-jinping-attends-meeting-with-chinese-private-sector-leaders.

63 Josephine Ma, 'Safeguarding China's Regime is the Top Priority, Xi Jinping Tells Politburo', *South China Morning Post*, 1 March 2025, scmp.com/news/china/politics/article/3300677/safeguarding-chinas-regime-top-priority-xi-jinping-tells-politburo.

64 Laura Silver and Christine Huang, 'Key Facts about China's Declining Population', Pew Research Center, 5 December 2022, pewresearch.org/short-reads/2022/12/05/key-facts-about-chinas-declining-population/.

One does not see long lines outside Chinese embassies of people seeking visas to migrate to China. If anything, the flow is the other way – out of China. Nor is it certain that even if substantial numbers of say, Laotians or Cambodians wanted to immigrate to China, Beijing would welcome them. Anyone can be Singaporean or Australian or American or French. But you are either Chinese or not. There are approximately 60 million overseas Chinese globally, according to UNESCO (unesco.org/en/articles/overseas-chinese-long-history-0). Even if every single one of them could be persuaded to migrate to China, it will not be enough to reverse China's population decline. In my view, the only source of foreign labour that would find China attractive may be Central Asians, but Beijing would not want them in China. Beijing never has had to think seriously about a foreign labour policy because of its reserves of rural labour and internal migration from rural China to the cities. But rural China is ageing too.

65 See 'Not One was Man Enough', *China Digital Space*, chinadigitaltimes.net/space/Not_one_was_man_enough.

66 Fei Xiaotong, *From the Soil: The Foundations of Chinese Society*, translation, (University of California Press, 1992).

67 The BRI is certainly ambitious in the scope of its vision. But vision and ambition are not reality, and the BRI was never more than a diverse collection of projects wrapped up in a slogan and touted as a strategy. But it is too incoherent to be a strategy. There is not even a single, definitive, publicly available official list of all BRI projects. As can be expected with such a motley collection of projects, some have worked better than others, some have been scaled down, some have stalled,

and some have failed. China has ceased to loudly boast about the BRI and the tone of Chinese BRI summits has become more subdued.

68 See memorandum from Secretary of State Rogers to President Nixon in 'Memorandum from the President's Assistant for National Security Affairs (Kissinger) to President Nixon', 10 September 1969 history.state.gov/historicaldocuments/frus1969-76v12/d88.

69 See Wang Hui, *China from Empire to Nation-State*, (Harvard University Press, 2014); Ge Zhaoguang, *What is China? Territory, Ethnicity, Culture, & History*, (Harvard University Press, 2018); and Wang Gungwu, *Renewal: The Chinese State and the New Global History*, (The Chinese University of Hong Kong, 2018).

70 Arthur M. Schlesinger Jr, *The Disuniting of America: Reflections on a Multicultural Society*, (W.W. Norton, 1991). A revised and expanded edition was issued in 1998.

71 See Bilahari Kausikan, 'Polarity is What States Make of It', in the compilation by various authors entitled 'The Long Unipolar Moment? Debating American Dominance', *Foreign Affairs*, November/December 2023, foreignaffairs.com/responses/long-unipolar-moment-american-dominance.

72 '66 pct of S. Koreans Support Developing Own Nuclear Weapons: Poll', Yonhap News Agency, 27 June 2024, m-en.yna.co.kr/view/AEN20240627011200315.

73 See Mark Fitzpatrick, *Asia's Latent Nuclear Powers: Japan, South Korea and Taiwan*, (Routledge and IISS, 2016).

74 'Japan's Plutonium Stockpile Climbs to 46.1 Tons in 2020, First Rise in 3 Years', *Mainichi Japan*, 10 July 2021, mainichi.jp/english/articles/20210710/p2a/00m/0na/018000c.

75 Jan Cienski and Wojciech Kość, 'Poland Seeks Access to Nuclear Arms and Looks to Build Half-Million-Man Army', *Politico*, 7 March 2025, politico.eu/article/donald-tusk-plan-train-poland-men-military-service-russia/.

76 Jesse Johnson, 'Japan Should Consider Hosting US Nuclear Weapons, Abe Says', *The Japan Times*, 27 February 2022, japantimes.co.jp/news/2022/02/27/national/politics-diplomacy/shinzo-abe-japan-nuclear-weapons-taiwan/.

Lowy Institute Penguin Specials

1. *Beyond the Boom*, John Edwards (2014)
2. *The Adolescent Country*, Peter Hartcher (2014)
3. *Condemned to Crisis*, Ken Ward (2015)
4. *The Embarrassed Colonialist*, Sean Dorney (2016)
5. *Fighting with America*, James Curran (2016)
6. *A Wary Embrace*, Bobo Lo (2017)
7. *Choosing Openness*, Andrew Leigh (2017)
8. *Remaking the Middle East*, Anthony Bubalo (2018)
9. *America vs the West*, Kori Schake (2018)
10. *Xi Jinping: The Backlash*, Richard McGregor (2019)
11. *Our Very Own Brexit*, Sam Roggeveen (2019)
12. *Man of Contradictions*, Ben Bland (2020)
13. *Reconstruction*, John Edwards (2021)
14. *Morrison's Mission*, Paul Kelly (2022)
15. *Rise of the Extreme Right*, Lydia Khalil (2022)
16. *Modern Warfare*, Sir Lawrence Freedman (2023)
17. *Best Laid Plans*, Sean Turnell (2024)
18. *India in a World Adrift*, Shivshankar Menon (2025)

INDIA IN A WORLD ADRIFT

Shivshankar Menon

A LOWY INSTITUTE PAPER

The pace of change in Asian geopolitics is accelerating. What role will India play in a rebalanced Asian system?

This book, by one of India's most senior and respected foreign policy minds, examines this moment of flux, and argues that we should prepare for dimming economic prospects and rival power blocs. What is the outlook for India in such a world, including its increasingly close relationship with Australia? Shivshankar Menon argues that India will work ever more closely with the West as part of New Delhi's broader quest for strategic autonomy.

BEST LAID PLANS

Sean Turnell

A LOWY INSTITUTE PAPER

The first in-depth account of the economic reform program of Myanmar's ill-fated Aung San Suu Kyi government, by one of her key advisers.

Best Laid Plans is a unique first-hand account of the radical economic reforms implemented in Myanmar under the ill-fated civilian government of Daw Aung San Suu Kyi. These reforms, designed both to turn around Myanmar's dire economy and lay the economic foundations for democracy, were brought to a dramatic end following the military coup in Myanmar in February 2021. Written by one of Suu Kyi's key economic advisers who was imprisoned alongside her in the wake of the coup, *Best Laid Plans* explores the nature of the reforms, the resistance they inspired, and the events that brought this all-too brief era of change to its catastrophic conclusion.

MODERN WARFARE

Sir Lawrence Freedman

A LOWY INSTITUTE PAPER

More than any other modern war, the fight between Russia and Ukraine has been a tough testing ground for modern weapons and operational concepts.

Drawing on extensive research into the conduct of the war during its first year, Sir Lawrence Freedman assesses the contrasting strategies of the two sides. Ukraine has fought along classical lines, seeking victory through battle. Russia has adopted a more total approach, combining conventional battles with attacks on Ukraine's socio-economic structure. Freedman explains why the apparently superior Russian force has been unable to defeat and subjugate Ukraine.

RISE OF THE EXTREME RIGHT

Lydia Khalil

A LOWY INSTITUTE PAPER

ASIO says right-wing extremism now makes up half its case load, and that it anticipates a terrorist attack on Australian soil within the year. There has been a 250 per cent increase in right-wing terrorism globally. So what exactly is right-wing extremism and how is its potential for violence growing? Why is it a global problem? How does it threaten democracy and what should we do about it? *Rise of the Extreme Right* answers these questions while situating Australia within the global threat landscape.

MORRISON'S MISSION

Paul Kelly

A LOWY INSTITUTE PAPER

When he became Prime Minister in 2018, Scott Morrison was a foreign policy amateur confronted by unprecedented challenges: an assertive Beijing and a looming rivalry between the two biggest economies in world history, the United States and China. Morrison plunged into foreign and security policy by making highly contentious changes that will be felt for decades, not least the historic decision to build nuclear-powered submarines.

Featuring interviews with Morrison and members of his cabinet, this book tells the story of the Prime Minister's foreign policy convictions and calculations, and what drove his attitudes towards China, America and the Indo-Pacific.

Powered by Penguin

Looking for more great reads, exclusive content and book giveaways?

Subscribe to our weekly newsletter.

Scan the QR code or visit penguin.com.au/signup